The Copyright Book

William S. Strong

**The Copyright Book:
A Practical Guide**

Second edition

The MIT Press
Cambridge, Massachusetts
London, England

This book was set in Palatino by
The MIT Press Computergraphics
Department and printed and bound
by Halliday Lithograph in the United
States of America.

Library of Congress Cataloging in
Publication Data

Strong, William S.
    The copyright book.

    Includes bibliographical references
and index.
    1. Copyright—United States. I.
Title.
KF2994.S75
1984   346.7304'82   84–7925
ISBN 0–262–19234–9   347.306482

For my parents

Contents

Preface to the Second Edition
ix

Preface
xi

1
The Subject Matter of Copyright
1

2
Ownership
24

3
Transfers of Copyright
41

4
Protecting Copyright
57

5
Registration of a Copyright Claim
72

6
Rights in Copyrighted Works
90

7
The Compulsory Licenses
101

8
Infringement and Fair Use
113

9
Works Created Before 1978
141

10
Tax Treatment of Copyrights
163

11
International Copyright Protection
and the Manufacturing Clause
173

Afterword
180

Appendixes
A. Methods of Affixation and
Positions of the Copyright Notice
on Various Types of Works
183

B. Form TX
191

C. "Best Edition" of Published
Copyrighted Works for
the Collections of the Library
of Congress
193

D. Registration of Computer
Programs and Data Bases
195

E. Warnings of Copyright for Use
by Certain Libraries and Archives
197

Notes
199

Index
217

Preface to the Second Edition

Since this book first appeared in the middle of 1981, a great many changes have occurred in the law of copyright. Recent opinions have clarified some issues in the law and muddied others. Some of those changes have attracted a good deal of attention. Not only the roller-coaster fate of home videotaping, but also the more abstruse questions of copyright as applied to computer software, have garnered newspaper headlines and weekly magazine coverage.

Of the two, computer software copyright is by far the more important, and perplexing, question. I have significantly expanded my treatment of the subject, with a view to telling you where matters stand as of press time, and also what unresolved issues remain that present, in my view, the greatest difficulties.

I have also taken the opportunity of this revision to expand my discussion of some matters that seemed, in retrospect, to deserve lengthier treatment than they received the first time around, and to explicate a few passages that puzzled earlier readers. I am grateful for the many comments I have received, whether praiseful or, as they say, "constructive." My aim will always be to make this book as useful, accurate, and current as I know how. You provide me the incentive, and you should reap the benefit.

Preface

At their best, our laws embody our deepest assumptions about human beings and what proper relations among human beings ought to be. Copyright is such a law. It springs from the belief that those who try to contribute to our always inadequate store of information and inspiration ought to be paid for their pains. This seems a very creditable attitude.

My purpose in writing this book has been to make available to people whose lives and work are affected by the laws of copyright an understanding of their rights and responsibilities. However, I hope that in doing so I have also managed to communicate some of my own fascination with the subject.

A new copyright law came into effect on January 1, 1978, overturning much that had gone before. It has enormous implications for authors and artists, not only in traditional media but in computer programming and other new areas of communication technology as well. It has equally great impact on those who use copyrighted works: teachers, performers, librarians, business people. So from both points of view, the time seems ripe for this project.

I have found it useful to write much of this book as though from the standpoint of the creator of a work—

be it a novel, a painting, a blueprint, a dance. But whatever is not kept safe for the artist is given to the public; if you are a would-be user of an artistic or other creative work, you will know your boundaries by the boundaries drawn for the creator of it.

I have tried to gather material and organize it in a way that will tell the story simply. This has not proved possible in all respects; parts of the law are so complex that no amount of pruning and rearranging could make them any less dense. Nor has it proved possible at every point to avoid technical language and terms whose legal definition differs from their ordinary meaning. In such places I have given examples to try to make clear what is being said.

Two further comments about organization are in order. First, because the new copyright law governs all works created after 1977 and many aspects of works created earlier, I have used the new law as my guide for most of this book. If you are concerned with pre-1978 works you should be sure to read chapter 9, which deals with these works. Second, although many rules differ from one art form to another, it became apparent that to deal with various art forms individually would create a great deal of needless repetition. Instead, therefore, I have treated the various aspects of the law as units and within each unit discussed the exceptions pertaining to one art form or another. It may be helpful to see the exceptions set out in this manner.

Space does not permit me to acknowledge adequately the encouragement of family and friends in the writing of this book. However, I do want to take the occasion to thank the staff at my former firm, Herrick & Smith, without whom all encouragement would have been in vain. In particular, I wish to thank Evie Hanlon and the Word Processing Crew, whose skill and patience were beyond measure.

The Copyright Book

1

The Subject Matter of Copyright

Copyright law is essentially a system of property. Like property in land, you can sell it, leave it to your heirs, donate it, or lease it under any sort of conditions; you can divide it into separate parts; you can protect it from almost every kind of trespass. Also, like property in land, copyrights can be subjected to certain kinds of public use that are considered to be in the public interest. I shall explain these various aspects of copyright property through the course of this book.

The province of copyright is communication. It does not deal with machines or processes—those are governed by patent law—or with titles, slogans, and the other symbols that businesses use to distinguish themselves in the public eye, for that is the stuff of trademark law. Works of art and literature are what copyright protects, no matter what the medium, and works whose purpose is to convey information or ideas. In the words of the statute, it protects "original works of authorship fixed in any tangible medium of expression, now known or later developed, from which they can be perceived, reproduced, or otherwise communicated, either directly or with the aid of a machine or device."[1]

This seemingly simple bit of language incorporates three of the fundamental concepts of the law, concepts whose meaning must be clearly grasped before all else: fixation, originality, and expression.

Fixation

Fixation is the act of rendering a creation in some tangible form in which, or by means of which, other people can perceive it. Even the word *perceive* has its special legal meaning; in the law's definition, one "perceives" a work of choreography, for example, or a work of music, by seeing on a piece of paper the notation that enables a performer to reproduce the work. Thus a musical work may be fixed in sheet music, as well as on tape. On the other hand, performing the musical work, without taping it simultaneously, does not fix it because the performance is not tangible. It is heard and is gone.

The great importance of the act of fixation is that it marks the beginning of your federal copyright. You obtain copyright under the federal law as of the instant that you fix your work in tangible form. Fixation also draws the boundary line between federal copyright protection and so-called common law copyright, which is largely the prerogative of the individual states. (*Common law* is the term for law that is built up over the years by judicial opinions; in the copyright field there has not been a great deal of variation from one state to another.)

Until January 1, 1978, common law copyright protected all unpublished works except those that were registered with the U.S. Copyright Office; now it protects only works that have not been fixed in tangible form.[2] If, for example, you have developed a pantomime in your head but have not written any notes about it that would enable another performer to reproduce it, your unfixed work falls under the protection of common law copyright. You may perform it as often as you like, or you can let others perform it for a fee, and no one else may copy it. Presumably, also, you can bequeath the right to perform it to your children, and they to their children. After your death, though, it will grow increasingly more difficult to prove just what your common law copyright consisted of and who owns it.

Not much more of substance can be said at this point about common law copyright. Rights in works that have not been fixed are difficult to prove and difficult to protect; it is not even easy to prove what the work is if there is no tangible copy of it. Because the new federal law has so severely restricted the operation of the common law, this book is devoted to works that are fixed and thus governed by the federal law, except where I specifically state otherwise.

Originality

The law requires that a work be the product of your own mind in order to be copyrightable. Originality is not by itself sufficient; facts, even if they are facts that no one else has ever discovered, are regarded as the common property of all of us, as are scientific discoveries, mathematical equations, and historical theories.[3] Facts are not copyrightable because they are not human inventions; theories are not copyrightable because they are ideas, not expression. But although originality is not sufficient in itself, it is essential all the same.

The law follows a highly subjective theory of originality that often surprises, and sometimes shocks, those encountering it for the first time. If asked whether a person can get a copyright for something that has been created by someone else, most people would answer "no," but that answer would not always be correct. It is true that you cannot get a valid copyright in material that you have taken from someone else's work. But if you have recreated a preexisting work without having had access to it or knowledge of it, you can enforce your copyright against anyone who has actually copied from you, regardless of the fact that that person might have copied with equal ease from the preexisting work. This conundrum is a great favorite of copyright scholars. "If by some magic," they say, "a man who had never known it were to compose anew Keat's Ode on a Grecian Urn, he would be an 'author,' and . . . others might not copy that poem, though they might of course copy Keats's."[4] It is said to illustrate the difference between copyright and patent (which is based on objective originality), and indeed it does. Whether at its extremes that difference should be a source of embarassment rather than pride is unclear.

That elements of your work may be in the public domain does not invalidate your entire copyright. It only limits your copyright to what is original with you.

An original exposition of public domain material may take the form of arrangement. For example, *The Waste Land* is clearly a copyrightable poem, even though many of its lines are taken from works that are in the public domain. Eliot's originality lies in the juxtaposition of these public domain elements, and his copyright extends only to the limit of his originality. Similarly, a collage of newspaper clippings is a copyrightable arrangement.

Of a slightly different nature, but copyrightable on the same basic principle, are works the law calls "derivative works." Derivative works are those in which someone else's creation is "recast, transformed, or adapted."[5] Translations, sound recordings that transform musical or other works into magnetic notation, movie versions of plays or stories, orchestrations of melodies, and dolls based on cartoon characters are all obvious examples of derivative works. Others are less obvious but equally common, such as art reproductions. A mezzotint reproduction of a painting might seem to be a copy rather than a derivative work entitled to a protection in its own right, but in fact it is regarded as a derivative work. The reasoning behind this is that the manufacture of an art reproduction in a medium different from that of the original requires the reproducer to contribute some measure of his own special skill, and that contribution is entitled to protection. In fact, it has even been held that an exact reproduction of a piece of sculpture, substantially reduced in scale, can be copyrighted as a derivative work if the making of it requires great artistic skill and effort.[6]

A derivative work may be made of a copyrighted work or of a work in the public domain. If it is of a copyrighted work and if the artist has not authorized it, the work will constitute an infringement of the artist's copyright. In any event, the protection afforded to a derivative work extends only to the original contribution of the maker.[7]

Would Eliot's *The Waste Land* be regarded as a derivative work? Would *West Side Story* be regarded as a derivative work of *Romeo and Juliet*? Would Moussorgsky's *Pictures at an Exhibition* be regarded as a derivative work of the pictures that inspired him? The answer to all three of these questions is "no." It may be helpful to analyze why.

Partly the question is one of motive. Eliot's use of preexisting poems was not intended to recast those works in another medium but to use them, through parody and juxtaposition, as building blocks for a message uniquely his own. It was not Eliot's intent, nor was it his achievement, merely to create a new version of Marvell's *To His Coy Mistress* when he wrote:

But at my back from time to time I hear
The sound of horns and motors which shall bring
Sweeney to Mrs. Porter in the spring.

Similarly, *West Side Story* is not based upon *Romeo and Juliet* in the way that the movie *Gone with the Wind* was based upon Margaret Mitchell's novel; it attempts not to tell Shakespeare's story in another medium but to tell its own story, which resembles Shakespeare's play in many important respects. (If *Romeo and Juliet* were still under copyright, *West Side Story* would be an infringement, but that is another matter.)

Partly, too, the question is one of recognizability. Quite simply, one does not recognize particular pictures in Moussorgsky's composition. Recognizability is not, perhaps, a firm and reassuring principle, but it is nonetheless an important one in determining derivativeness.

Another category of derivative works that deserves mention is that described in the statute as works "consisting of editorial revisions, annotations, elaborations, or other modifications which, as a whole, represent an original work of authorship." What the law protects here is the original contribution of the editor or annotator. The law will not protect trivial modifications, but it will protect modifications that are sweeping enough to constitute a "new version" of the preexisting work. The protection given a revision would cover only the work of the editor's own creativity. If a scholar, on the basis of research, revises the text of, say, a poem by Spenser, he cannot get a copyright in the new text because what he has done is to restore Spenser's own words.

The amount of originality required for a derivative work to be eligible for copyright is not as clear-cut as my earlier mention of mezzotints and reduced-scale sculptures might suggest. Recent cases have shown a tightening of the rules, with results that may in the end prove unfortunate. The same court (the Second Circuit Court of Appeals) that in 1951 upheld the copyright of mezzotints struck down, in 1976, the copyright of an Uncle Sam mechanical bank that was a smaller-scale version of earlier, public domain models but with certain features altered. In 1980, it denied copyright to three-dimensional models of cartoon characters. And in 1983, another federal court (the Seventh Circuit) denied copyright to paintings that were based on movie stills. At present only one Court of Appeals still holds to the more liberal standard of earlier cases; when last heard from on this subject, in 1962, the Ninth Circuit was willing to grant copyright to a three-dimensional plastic Santa Claus and protect it at least against slavish copying.[8] In 1951, all that was required for copyright was that the author have contributed a "distinguishable variation"; in 1984, at least for some courts, the variation must also be "substantial." This new substantiality requirement is out of synch with the general standard of originality that applies elsewhere in the law.

Those judges who have taken the more restrictive view seem particularly worried that a looser standard will make it difficult in litigation to determine which work was being copied, the original or the derivative. Also, they seem to fear the creation of traps by those who slyly place copyright notices on works to which they have made covert alterations. These fears seem to me exaggerated. If we apply the "distinguishable variation" test, it will be easy to know whether a defendant has copied the original or the derivative work by whether the variation appears in the defendant's product. As for traps, two things can be said. First, if the variation is truly distinguishable, forcing the would-be copyist to go to the original source does not seem all that oppressive.[9] Second, those who set such traps can always (and usually should) be punished by the courts when the traps are sprung in litigation, by granting attorneys' fees to the defendants.

The substantiality doctrine will, if taken too far, make it impossible for one who adapts a work to a new medium to get a copyright without making changes in the content of the work as well. At the moment, that is not an immediate danger. But it does seem that, as things stand now, an adaptation of a work to another medium, or to a larger or smaller scale, will be most likely to obtain copyright if it either requires great artistic skill and labor to make or substantially varies from the original.

What about editorial revisions by a publisher? As a general rule, a publisher's revisions of an author's manuscript are not extensive enough to qualify as a derivative work. Indeed, such a result would go against the meaning of most publishing contracts. However, if a publishing contract specifically calls for major editing, the author should insist that his publisher specifically disclaim any rights in its editorial product.

Authors should always bear in mind that the right to creative derivative works is part of copyright. Thus, if an author transfers all rights in a work to someone else, this right goes with the rest. The author would no longer be able, for example, to create new versions of his work. If this is not desirable, the author should insist on the contract being changed.

The law's protection of art reproductions as derivative works illustrates, perhaps in an extreme way, its regard for originality, wherever found. But the law also protects, within the category known as "compilations" (which comprises everything from *The Oxford Book of English Verse* to the *Yellow Pages*), a vast number of works that have no originality whatever: airline guides, telephone directories, catalogs, and so on.[10] What is really being protected in such cases is the economic value of the work put into them. The scope of the copyright is understandably narrow. If you put out, say, a catalog of the works of a painter, which contains lists almost identical to someone else's, you are not necessarily infringing copyright in the earlier catalogue. You will be held liable only if you have taken a free ride on the first writer's labor; if as a result of your own investigations you arrive at the same results, you will be able to get your own copyright.[11] Where you are using the first writer's work as a data base for making a compilation that might be called a "derivative work" of the earlier work, the courts will generally require that you go to the trouble of independently verifying the data you use.

When a derivative work gets its own copyright, this copyright is limited, like all other copyrights, to whatever material is original with the creator. An English translation of *Anna Karenina* is a derivative work, and it can be copyrighted, but the copyright will be narrowly defined to avoid giving the translator any kind of rights in what was actually created by Tolstoy. The translator will be protected against someone who copies his translation but not against someone who makes a similar translation by independent effort. Another example would be the musical version of *Oliver Twist*. Without doubt the musical *Oliver* is copyrightable, but only to the extent that its characters, its plot, and its dialogue differ from Dickens's novel and are the original creation of its authors. You are at liberty, if it strikes your fancy, to write another musical based on *Oliver Twist*, but you cannot use the variations from Dickens's story that the authors of *Oliver* created, unless they are variations absolutely necessary to the task and unavoidable.

If the derivative work you make is of a work still subject to copyright, much the same rules applies. Your copyright in your derivative work covers only your own inventions, variations, and additions. You have no right to authorize someone else to use those parts of your derivative work that you have taken from the original.[12] For example, if you obtain a license to create a new edition of a copyrighted book, you can permit someone to publish your version as such, for that is implicit in your license, but you have no right to publish only those parts of it that you took from the original. Nor can you, without authority from the original copyright owner, permit someone else to make yet another revised edition of what is not original with you. Furthermore, when the copyright term of the original work runs out, everything in your work that you took from the original goes into the public domain, and only what you yourself have created will remain protected.

Tracing a work through its derivative forms can be like tagging migratory animals. Take the example of the movie *South Pacific*. It started out as a collection of short stories by James Michener. Next, several of the stories were combined and adapted into a musical by Rodgers and Hammerstein. Then the musical was rewritten as a screenplay, and the screenplay was made into a movie. There were thus three layers of derivative works, each cutting old material and adding new. And the movie producer had three different copyrights to worry about: the novel, the musical, and the screenplay. The movie could not be made, in fact, without derivative work licenses covering all three previous forms.

Expression   The third requirement of copyrightability is that the work be "expression" and not "idea." It is an old truism in copyright law that you cannot copyright an idea, but only your expression of it: ideas, like facts, are in the public domain. For example, a literary critic who publishes a new theory of the structure of the novel cannot obtain a copyright in that theory; he can copyright only his written expression of that theory. A thief may steal his theory with impunity if the thief expresses the theory in his own words, and the thief, scurrilous though he may be, can obtain a new copyright in his own written work.

A simple example like this may make the rule itself seem simple. It is not. In fact, it is riddled with ambiguities. What, for example, is a musical "idea" and how is it separable from musical "expression"? How basic must a plot become, how stripped of embellishment, before it ceases to be the writer's own copyrightable expression and becomes mere "idea"? No one really knows the answers to these questions, though many a court has formulated an all-embracing theory, only to see it discarded by the next court.

The rule that an idea cannot be copyrighted has an interesting corollary: copyright in the expression of an idea will not be enforced so as to prevent other people from putting the idea to practical use. This principle was first stated in the last century, in the case of *Baker v. Selden*, which involved a book on accounting techniques.[13] The book described a system of bookkeeping and, as illustration of it, contained a page ruled into columns appropriate for the system. When another publisher, impressed by the system, printed and sold copies of the ruled page—without any explanatory material—the original author brought suit.

In a decision that has continued to reverberate through the case law ever since, the Supreme Court held for the defendant. It said that if a copyrighted work describes a system or process, copyright does not prevent anyone else from making whatever printed works are necessary to use that system. To hold otherwise, the Court said, would be to treat the copyright like a patent.

It is important to understand the limits of this principle. *Baker v. Selden* does not stand for the proposition that blank forms cannot be copyrighted. It does mean, though, that forms will not be protected if protection would prevent other people from using the system they embody. Nor does *Baker v. Selden* apply to forms that are purely arbitrary in their content, such as the answer sheets for copyrighted tests.[14]

In recent years, the rule of *Baker v. Selden* has been applied to insurance contracts and other works that have a business or commercial use. The rule is that if a certain order of words is the only reasonable way, or one of only a few reasonable ways, of putting an idea to use, that precise order of words will be protected only narrowly, or not protected at all.[15]

Under certain circumstances, an idea may be protected prior to publication by an agreement to treat it as confidential. (Confidentiality is part of the law of trade secrets, and is not a part of the copyright law.) If you wish to submit an idea for a work, or for an advertising program, or something of the sort, make every effort to get a written or at least oral agreement in advance from whomever you wish to submit it to that it will be treated in confidence and paid for if used. In the absence of such an agreement, the other person will probably not be obligated to pay you. You will have only yourself to blame if you blurt out your idea without getting this protection.

One possible approach, though I have not yet seen it used in practice, might be to submit the idea in a sealed envelope, along with a covering letter stating that the enclosed proposal is submitted in confidence. Opening the envelope would be interpreted as acceptance of your confidentiality requirement. Like any other technique, this one will work only with companies that are willing to deal with outsiders—and many companies no longer are.

Scope of Copyright   Once the three basic requirements of fixation, originality, and expression are met, the law's protection, though not universal, is extremely broad. Almost any kind of artistic work or work that communicates a message in any tangible medium can be copyrighted. The statute specifically lists literary works (a term that means practically any printed work), musical works (including accompanying words), dramatic works (including accompanying music), pantomimes, choreographic works, "pictorial, graphic and sculptural works" (in other words, any visual work, whether two- or three-dimensional), sound recordings, motion pictures and all other audiovisual works—and this list is not complete.[16] None of these categories implies artistic merit; the telephone directory is considered a "literary work," and roadmaps are "graphic works."[17]

Performances of works are not regarded as works themselves until they are fixed, on tape or film, as sound recordings or audiovisual works. They are therefore not protected by copyright law until that time. This does not mean that someone can film or record a performance without the performer's permission, for that is forbidden by other laws.[18] Whether it means that someone can imitate that performer's interpretation or style is a matter on which the courts have not agreed.[19]

Although the law does not require that a work have artistic merit, certain works nonetheless do stand outside its shelter, in the cold drizzle of uncopyrightability. They are excluded for one of two reasons: either they are trivial, or they are utilitarian.

In the first category fall, for example, titles and slogans, and minor variations upon works already in the public domain.[20] Titles and slogans can be protected to some extent by federal trademark law and by state laws against unfair competition and misappropriation; a title, for example, will be protected by those laws if it has acquired such a reputation in the public mind that the use of it by someone else would amount to taking a free ride on the first user's popularity.[21] This protection, though, exists entirely apart from copyright, and is not available for most items that are excluded from copyright on the grounds of triviality. Ballroom or discotheque dance steps, for example, are not considered to rise to the level of choreographic works within the meaning of the copyright statute, and are unlikely to find protection under any other legal doctrine.[22]

The exclusion of utilitarian works is considerably less simple a concept. A typeface is not copyrightable as a pictorial or graphic work because Congress feels that typefaces are fundamentally utilitarian—that is, the purpose of their existence is to produce other things. There is every reason to believe that this interpretation applies equally well to calligraphic alphabets not intended as typefaces. An illuminated letter is clearly copyrightable as a pictorial work, but someone's personal variation of the uncial alphabet would probably not be. Anyone could use that alphabet in making other works, although the calligrapher's actual writings could not be printed and sold without permission.

As one explores the concept that utilitarian aspects of design are not copyrightable, it grows more difficult to find one's way. Congress has said that elements of utilitarian articles that "can be identified separately from the useful article as such"—that is, elements that are not functional—are copyrightable.[23] One almost needs training in Platonic philosophy to be able to make this sort of distinction. One is being asked, in essence, to discuss the lampness of a lamp, the tableness of a table. I bid you look up from this book for a moment at the lamp beneath which you are reading and identify those parts of its design that may clearly be segregated from its functional requirements. If your lamp is by Tiffany, your task will be relatively easy; if, on the other hand, it is made in the Scandinavian style, the problem is rather more challenging.

Does this mean that if a lamp cannot be copyrighted, a drawing cannot be either? Not so. Even a drawing by a lamp designer, made not as an end in itself but solely as a prelude to manufacture, is copyrightable as a pictorial work, because it is not in itself a useful article but only teaches how to make one. No one may publish copies of the drawing without the designer's permission.[24] However, the copyright does not prevent someone from actually making a lamp that embodies the functional parts portrayed in the drawing. (Here again you hear the echo of *Baker v. Selden*.) The designer's right to control manufacture based on his drawing extends only to those parts of his drawing that depict nonfunctional things.[24]

Architectural works present a special difficulty. An architect's plans, like any other drawings, are copyrightable as pictorial or graphic works. No one may publish those drawings without the architect's permission. However, so far as the functional, utilitarian elements depicted by those drawings are concerned, anyone who sees the blueprints can erect a building incorporating those elements, and the architect cannot stop him.[25]

What about the building itself, once it is built? As a rule, buildings are not copyrightable. But the law does provide that "nonfunctional" or "monumental" structures are copyrightable as sculptural works.[26] What do *nonfunctional* and *monumental* mean? The pyramids are now regarded as monuments, but when they were built they were perceived as functional. The Committee Report for the Copyright Act says that copyright will not cover elements of shape in a building that are "conceptually inseparable from the utilitarian aspects of the structure," a distinction that may prove as difficult to make in practice as in the example of the Scandinavian lamp.[27]

Plots and Characters

In any given work, the coverage afforded by copyright is broader than you might think, primarily because more and more things that long ago were considered merely ideas have come to be regarded as expression. For example, the plot of a novel is covered by the novel's copyright, at least to the extent that it is original with the author. The courts have developed the ingenious theory that a plot is an "arrangement of ideas" and that an arrangement of ideas amounts, magically, to "expression."[28] From a philosophical or logical point of view, this is probably a falsehood, but nonetheless it is the law.

What about characters? Here, again, the law gives protection to what might at first seem to be an idea. Indeed similarity of characters is often the principal battleground when one author sues another for plagiarism. But there is one unusually perplexing problem with characters: who owns them? (You may as well resign yourself early to one of the facts of life of copyright law: no principle is fixed or firm, self-defining or self-limiting. If you are a commonsensical sort of person, this will cause you frequent exasperation, but on the other hand, common sense will also tend to get you out of the mazes into which pure logic leads.)

This problem of characters arose in a case involving *The Maltese Falcon*.[29] After selling the story to Warner Brothers, Dashiell Hammett wrote several more stories about his detective hero, Sam Spade. Warner Brothers took him to court, claiming that he had violated the terms of his contract of sale and that the character, Sam Spade, was their exclusive property.

It might have been enough for the court to construe the contract in Hammett's favor and to hold that he had not, in fact, sold Warner Brothers his rights in Sam Spade. The court did this, but it did not let the matter rest there. It went on to consider whether a character, as such, could even be copyrighted, and concluded that it could not, unless it constituted the story being told. (Emma in Jane Austen's novel might be an example of the latter case.) Its opinion was that characters like Sam Spade are a writer's stock-in-trade and that the activities or words of a character in a particular story are copyrightable but not the character as such. The court characterized an author's ownership of a character as property of a different sort—property that is protected by ordinary legal rules, not by copyright law.

At first this seems a reasonable proposition. Certainly it helped the court decide the case for the right party. But the implications of this ruling, particularly under the new law, are far-reaching.

First, the court was wrong to say that characters are uncopyrightable. If someone other than Hammett himself had used Sam Spade, or a character just like Sam Spade but with a different name, Warner Brothers would have won. And the court would have said that use of Sam Spade was a violation of copyright; courts have said as much in hundreds of other cases. So it is clear that we are speaking here of a special property right for the benefit of the author.

But even admitting this, we still must face another question: how long does this unusual property right last? Does it vanish when the author dies, or can he bequeath it to his children? Can he bequeath it to someone who has no connection at all with his copyrights? Could Hammett, for example, have bequeathed his rights in Sam Spade to Lillian Hellman, and would Hammett's children and publishers then have been powerless to stop her from writing books about Sam Spade? (The court never faced these problems; I would not venture to guess how a court might decide them in the future.)

The final problem of this case is that it may mean that a sale by an author of his "property" in a character is not protected by the provision in the new law that permits an author to terminate (revoke) a transfer of copyright. I shall deal with termination at length in chapter 8; I raise the point now only to underscore the dangers presented by this view of the law.

It may well be that the *Maltese Falcon* case will be altered or simply ignored in the future. If it is, however, authors may suffer in new and different ways. My advice is that, if you wish to retain the right to license other publishers and producers to use your characters and your locale, you should specify that in any movie or publication contract. If you do so, you will be protected even if the *Maltese Falcon* rule is abandoned.

Computer Programs

Many principles of copyright are being put to the test as courts struggle with questions concerning computer programs. Programs are eligible for copyright, but there is considerable confusion about what such a copyright protects or should protect.

For the moment, the law is that a computer program is protected not only in source code form but in object code form as well. This is true even if the object code is embedded in the computer, as is the case with operating system software.[30] (Source code is the version of a program that is written in FORTRAN, PASCAL, C, or any of the other so-called "computer languages." The source code of a program is not intelligible to a layman but can be easily read and understood by experts. Object code, on the other hand, is the machine-readable form of a program, whether in tape, disk, or other form, and is intelligible for the most part only to the machine it is put into, not to humans. Operating system software is the set of instructions that governs the computer's thought processes, so to speak.) I say "for the moment," because there are real difficulties in this doctrine that have yet to be resolved.

At the time that this sensitive area was being studied by the National Commission on New Technological Uses of Copyrighted Works (CONTU), most Commission members felt that object code was merely a copy of the source code and should be protected by copyright. In a vigorous dissent, however, the novelist John Hersey and others protested that an object code, although it is an embodiment of the source code, functions solely as a part of the computer, is not intended to communicate to human beings, and should not be protected by copyright.[31] Thus, the dispute centered on what the copyright law means when it defines a "copy" as "a material object in which a work is fixed by any method now known or later developed, and from which the work can be perceived, reproduced, or otherwise communicated, either directly or with the aid of a machine or device." The majority of the Commission took the view that the object code of a program was a copy because, theoretically, the source code could be printed out from it. The fact is, however, that that is not the purpose of object code, and indeed the last thing any program vendor wants is for his program to be deciphered; most try (however futilely) to encrypt or otherwise protect their object codes from ever being "read" and understood.

In my opinion, the dissent held the higher ground, so far as logic is concerned. But logic is not the only force at work here; CONTU and the courts have, whether consciously or not, acted partly out of fear that not to extend copyright protection to object code will open the gates to the Japanese or Taiwanese invader. Certainly, that fear is widespread in the computer industry. Many computer people will, if pressed, admit that copyright doesn't fit very well onto object code, but, they say, patent protection is expensive and time-consuming to obtain, and most programs have only a short commercial life.

Yet, whether they like it or not, the rule that has so far been adopted by the courts has put copyright on a collision course with patent law. Indeed, a recent case has extended patent protection to a package of cash management software on the grounds that the program constitutes a patentable business system.[32] Now if a program is a patentable system, then it cannot also be a copyrightable work, because copyright is expressly denied to any "procedure, process, system, [or] method of operation."[33] The Supreme Court has yet to speak on this question, but it is noteworthy that it recently upheld a patent granted to a manufacturing process in which the only novel element was a relatively simple computer program.[34] As the field of robotics grows in importance, this conflict between patent and copyright will worsen, because a programmed robot is undeniably a machine, and to allow copyright to protect its unique aspects for fifty years or more, without requiring the inventor to meet the stringent tests of patentability, is flagrantly unfair.

What should you do in the meantime, if you have a piece of software ready to market? If you plan to distribute by one-on-one licensing, you would do well to follow common industry practice, and rely primarily on trade secret protection. Place tight restrictions on the uses that your customer can make of the software, prohibit disclosure to persons other than the licensee and certain of its employees, and require return or destruction of the software if for any reason the license is terminated. If you are marketing your software over the counter, trade secret protection is of course not available. However, you are probably safe relying on copyright at this stage. If it should ultimately be decided that copyright does not protect object code, Congress will almost certainly legislate some sort of relief.

So far as patent is concerned, one cannot deny that for most programs, which have a short market life, patent registration is too slow, expensive, and cumbersome. However, granting copyright protection to things like operating system software—to pick the most blatant example—is in effect granting a long term patentlike monopoly without requiring the inventor to meet the standards of patentability. This is not healthy for the economy, nor in the long run for the law either. A better solution may be to enact a special statute for software, combining elements of patent and copyright.

Another major issue of copyright in software has yet to be addressed by any court, namely, how we distinguish the "expression" in a program from the "idea." A program is fundamentally a series of instructions directing a computer to perform certain analytic or other functions. If the problem to be solved is a difficult one, writing the program requires great skill and creativity, and, we say at a gut level, this effort deserves protection. But how do we protect those instructions without actually protecting the process they embody? In the precomputer age, instructions for doing something, even something so arbitrary as playing a game, were narrowly limited in their copyrights.[35] CONTU considered this question, and decided that for any given data processing problem there were a great number of possible programming solutions. At a certain level of specificity, they said, the choice of computer instructions constitutes the "expression" of the general solution or algorithm, which in turn constitutes the idea.[36]

If this strikes you as disingenuous, I am inclined to agree. A process is no less a process just because it is set out in more detail or is chosen from a group of processes that have the same end result. CONTU's analysis likens a program to the plot of a novel, in which the arrangement of ideas can constitute expression. But the specifics of a plot are themselves a commentary on human life and as such constitute part of the novel's end result; it cannot be said that two plots, in their details, are merely two ways of getting from A to B, because the author's choice of details helps define and describe the world he is writing about. Furthermore, a novelist sitting down to write is not limited in his choice of plot, setting, or any of those other things that comprise expression, by the need to arrive at B. He has the whole world from which to choose his details, and if the choice leads him ultimately to C, so much the better: the muse is at work. A computer programmer, on the other hand, cannot choose details at random but must always have his eye on B, and is judged on his skill by how quickly and efficiently he gets there. ("Efficiently"—is that a word compatible with copyright?) Still, the CONTU theory has some validity, if only because there is no clear alternative. It will be interesting to see how the courts grapple with it.

Just to confuse matters a little further, I am told by many programmers that in their view the true commercial value of a program lies in the algorithm, not in the programming details. Any good programmer, they say, can take a piece of software and, using its basic structure, come up with a program that will do the same things in somewhat different ways. This puts us squarely in a dilemma, for we cannot protect against that sort of rearrangement without in effect protecting the ideas of the program.

Given these complexities, it is small wonder that no case has yet come up that forced a court to go through this sort of analysis. The cases to date involve outright, even brazen, appropriation of software. Only in the area of videogames has there been copying that was not verbatim, and those cases were dealt with by viewing the games as audiovisual works, so that the court could focus on more familiar visual copying.[37]

My message is not despair and confusion, although it may seem somewhat like that. I do think there are serious problems in this area. We are dealing with new wine and old bottles and need to be extremely cautious of the quick fix. It is regrettable that there has been so little public debate on these matters, for they will come to affect us all intimately.

Works Created with the Aid of Computers

Can a work created by applying a computer program to a data base receive a copyright? A typical work of this sort might be a Biblical concordance, created by feeding the Bible into a computer data bank and then applying to it a program designed to locate and arrange word correspondences. Although no one has yet raised the issue, there seems to be no reason why a work of this type should not be entitled to a copyright. Admittedly the computer is doing the bulk of the legwork, but this is only at the guidance of a human being. A certain degree of human will and intellectual labor is present in any computer product.

As intellectual production of this type becomes more and more common, some unusual problems of ownership will emerge. I shall deal with these in greater detail in the next chapter.

2 Ownership

Copyright comes into existence at the moment of a work's creation, just as, in some theologies, the soul enters the body at birth. At that time, ownership vests in the author or authors.

The word *author* has a special meaning in the copyright law. It is used regardless of the kind of work; writers, painters, sculptors, and composers are all authors. This usage, indeed, is almost universal—in other countries as a matter of convenience, and in this country as a necessity. The Constitution, from which Congress derives its power to establish copyrights, speaks specifically of "authors" and "writings," and in order to extend the law's protection to nonliterary works, the courts have had to interpret these words broadly. However, *author* is not synonymous with *creator*, for in certain circumstances a person, or company, will be considered an author without lifting a creative finger. So what seems at first almost a frivolous question— Who is the author?—is in fact both complex and important.

Authorship

Only in a work by one individual acting on his own behalf is the answer to the question obvious. In the case of, say, a poem written by one person and set to music by another, it is anything but obvious. Three different relationships can exist between that poet and that composer. The first, in which the words and music are considered separately, can hardly even be called a relationship. The poet is the author of the words and may do what he likes with his poem; the composer is the author of the music and may do with the music anything that he pleases. In the absence of some exclusive licensing arrangement, the first composer cannot prevent another from making a new musical setting for the poem, and the first poet cannot prevent another from writing new words to fit the music. A singer who wants to perform such a song would have to buy the performance right in the poem from the poet and the performance right in the music from the composer.

It is also possible, and more common, for the poet and composer to be "joint authors," and for the song to be a "joint work." Joint authorship ranks among the more slippery principles of copyright law, and many courts and committees have grappled with it without achieving a clear victory. Intuitively we all know what a joint work is; it is, just as the statute says, a work "prepared by two or more authors with the intention that their contributions be merged into inseparable or interdependent parts of a unitary whole."[1] But what do these words mean? Do they mean that for a work to be a joint work, all of the authors must agree among themselves before any of them begins creating any part of the work? That would violate good sense. As one court said in a case under the old law:

Suppose, for example, that after Burnett had composed the music, expecting his wife to write the words, she had died or changed her mind about writing the lyrics, and Burnett had gone to [his publisher] and asked him to find someone to write the words. We submit that no court would hold that the fact that when Burnett composed the music he expected his wife to write the words, would make the actual song any less a 'joint work' of Burnett and the lyricist found by [his publisher].[2]

The force of this reasoning cannot be denied, and I think there is little doubt that it will be applied to the new statute. In any event, there is no reason for requiring an initial agreement where a work is one in which the contributions of the various authors are "inseparable," as opposed to merely "interdependent." For example, if a painter begins a painting and when she is halfway done decides to collaborate with another painter in finishing it, the contributions are inseparable and the work is inescapably a joint work; no possible alternative designation exists. The time of the agreement in such a case is irrelevant.

The trouble, at least with works whose parts are merely "interdependent" (as words and music are in a song), is that once you abandon a strict requirement of a prior agreement, you have no sure footing anymore. Take an extreme case. Suppose a writer writes a book and lyrics, intending them to be a part of a musical comedy, but dies before finding a composer. Since the copyright term is the lifetime of the author plus fifty years, the writer's death supposedly starts the clock running. Suppose that, forty-nine years later, the author's heir finds a composer, who turns the book and lyrics into a musical comedy, just as the dead author had intended should happen. If this is considered a joint work, the copyright term in the whole thing—book, lyrics, and music—will be extended to the life of the composer plus fifty years, since the term of a joint work is based on the life of the last joint author to die.

Will this musical comedy in fact be considered a joint work? The statute does not say that an author's intention ends at death; all that seems to matter is the intention with which an author's contribution was created. The natural response is to say, "But that can't be what the law means!" That is probably correct. My example, however, is purposefully extreme. If the lapse of time between the writing of the lyrics and the writing of the music is only ten years, does the same result still outrage one's sense of logic? If the lapse is two years? Or say that the lyricist has not died but that he wrote his lyrics at age twenty and does not find a composer until he is eighty-five and on his deathbed. The problem is the same, though the circumstances differ superficially. What should be the result in such a case? Someone will have to win (and someone will have to lose) a lawsuit before we will know. It is unfortunate that this is so, because uncertainty of this kind in the law invariably leads to hardship for someone.

It might be possible to argue that if the lyricist is dead the musical comedy should be considered a derivative work instead of a joint work. The problem is, again, that the intention on which the law focuses is the intention with which the author's contribution was created.[3] If the lyricist's words are set to music during his lifetime, he can hardly claim that the result is a derivative work. Does death or the passage of time change all this?

Well, perhaps I have belabored the point long enough. This metaphysical problem, "Is there intent after death?", will probably not arise too often, and should not cause you undue alarm; the ordinary joint work is a creature of common sense. The problem will not arise at all in the case of works in which contributions are "inseparable." Suppose a painter dies leaving an unfinished canvas. If a collaborator was working on it at the time of the painter's death, he can continue to work on it, and the end product will be a joint work. Otherwise the canvas must be considered complete at the artist's death, and if the painter's heir arranges to have someone else to finish it, the result would have to be a new version of the work, a derivative work with a separate copyright.

Joint authors are called "tenants in common," a term borrowed from the law of real estate. This means that each of them owns an undivided share of the entire work. Not necessarily an equal share, for the authors can slice the pie unevenly if they so choose.[4] But because ownership is theoretically undivided, each of them can transfer rights in the work without consulting the others. (If he does so, he will have to account to his fellow authors for their shares of the profits.) However, a transfer of that sort will not prevent any of the other joint authors from making an identical sale to someone else, and for this reason, purchasers usually insist on getting all of the authors to sign the contract.

Outside the United States, a grant will not be effective unless signed by all joint authors, and anyone contemplating foreign distribution of a work will insist on obtaining all signatures.[5]

Works Made for Hire

I have discussed so far two possible relationships between persons whose creative efforts are in some manner connected. The first is that they are merely independent authors combining their independent creations; the second is that they are joint authors. The third possible relationship is that one of them is an employee of the other, in which case the resulting work is a "work made for hire." Works made for hire have a different copyright term from that of most other works, and they are the only works for which an author has no statutory right to terminate a transfer. (See the discussion of termination of rights in chapter 8.) The author of a work made for hire is the person who does the hiring; the creator has no rights whatever in the work.

The most obvious examples of works made for hire are newspapers, movies, dictionaries, and other works that we think of as created, in a sense, by the companies that publish them. These companies have staffs of full-time writers and artists who work specifically on these products.

The rule is broader though. An employer is considered the author of anything written by an employee within the scope of his employment. Thus when a scientist in a research laboratory writes a report on her work for her supervisor, the laboratory is the author of the report.

How can you tell if a person is an employee, within the meaning of the law? The clear-cut example is the full-time staff writer, who is an employee in every sense of the word. But what about someone who is hired for a single project, paid by the job—or not paid at all—and dismissed? The critical factor here would be the extent of the employer's control over the person's work. If the person works under supervision, he is likely to be considered an employee, even if he is a volunteer.[6] If the work is farmed out to him, though— as, for example, in the case of a company that commissions architectural plans or advertising materials— he is probably what the law calls an "independent contractor" and not an employee.

An interesting example of the importance of control is the case of university professors. From time to time universities have tried to assert copyright in faculty lectures. The courts have not agreed, and the crucial factor in their thinking seems to be that universities quite purposefully do not control the style or content of lectures.[7] This rationale would not, of course, apply to internal memoranda written for administrative purposes.

As you can see, there will be room for disagreement on the employee versus independent contractor question in many situations, but these examples should help to determine the answer in most cases.

Can you, as an employee, arrange for your work not to be considered "for hire?" Unfortunately not, if you are an employee in the usual sense of that word. The most you can do in advance is either agree that certain types of work will not be in the scope of employment, or agree that even if the employer is to be the author you will still own the rights, or certain specific rights, in the work. This amounts to a transfer in advance of copyright ownership. The first type of agreement may be written or oral; but written is more reliable. The latter type must be in writing and signed by both the employer and the employee; otherwise the agreement will be only a nonexclusive license to the employee.[8]

Under the old law, this was not so. Prior to publication, an author's entire copyright could be transferred orally, and this applied in the work for hire context as well.[9] By a handshake, an employer and employee could effectively waive the work for hire rule. Even now, the formality of requiring both signatures applies only to agreements between an employer and employee made in advance of creation of the work. After the work is in fact created, the normal rules for transfer of copyright apply. (See chapter 3.)

One special form of the work for hire rule relates to works of the U.S. Government. The law denies copyright to works "prepared by an officer or employee of the United States Government as part of that person's official duties."[10] (These works may nonetheless receive copyright protection in other countries.[11]) By implication, it seems probable that if a Government officer or employee, working within the scope of his official duties, jointly authors a work with a private citizen, the private citizen will own the entire copyright and have no obligation beyond the terms of his contract to share any of the profits with the Government. Will the Government have any rights? It is impossible to say, for the issue has never been tried.

Problems arise in defining a person's official duties. The well-publicized lawsuits involving President Nixon's and Henry Kissinger's tapes and memoranda are only the most sensational. By and large, though, the "scope of the employment" test will work here as with other works for hire.[12] What is less certain is whether the Government can waive its authorship rights, as a private employer can.

Without the work-made-for-hire doctrine, newspapers, magazines, and other businesses could not function. If a newspaper had to deal with hundreds of copyright contracts every day, the burden and cost would be oppressive. Nonetheless the doctrine does deprive many creative people of the chance to reap the full rewards of their work. For this reason, the law creates a presumption that a work is not made for hire unless the creator really is employed to do that sort of work. This brings us to the question of commissioned or specially-ordered works.

Until January 1, 1978, almost any commissioned work, even one made on a one-time commission, could be considered a work made for hire, depending on the intent of the people involved. As a general rule, for example, commissioned portraits were works for hire, and the copyright belonged to the purchaser instead of the painter.[13] Under the new law, only certain types of commissioned works can be treated as works made for hire, and then only if the creator and the person or entity commissioning the work agree that this is to be the case. Outside of these situations, the initial copyright in a commissioned work will belong to the creator regardless of whatever agreement may be made.

Commissioned works that may be treated as works made for hire are these:

• A contribution to a movie or other audiovisual work.
• A contribution to a periodical or other collective work.
• A translation.
• A supplementary work, that is, a work that is somehow auxiliary to the main work—for example, an illustration, an illustrative map or chart, editorial notes, a musical arrangement, a bibliography, a foreword, an index, and so forth—but only if it is subordinate to the main work. For example, illustrations that are of equivalent importance to the text will not qualify as subordinate works.
• A compilation, that is, a work created by collecting and assembling data or preexisting materials; an example would be an anthology, a hotel guide, or a racing chart.
• An instructional text.
• A test or answer material for a test.
• An atlas.

For any of these commissioned works to be a work made for hire, the creator and whoever commissions him must agree that this will be so. The agreement must be in writing and signed by both of them. The law does not require in so many words that the contract has to say, "This work will be a work made for hire," but there is little doubt that that is what it means. The presumption of the law goes so strongly against treating commissioned works as being made for hire that a court is likely to interpret any language less explicit than this in the opposite way. Even if the contract says, "*A* hires *B* to do such-and-such," a court may well believe that the word *hires* was used loosely as a synonym for *commissions*. The phrase *work made for hire* is a legal term and ought to be used wherever that is the intent.

By the same token, any agreement that a person who is doing work for hire will have any exclusive rights in that work must also be in writing and signed by both parties.[14]

To be commissioned, a work must be done at the request of the person for whom it is done. Nevertheless some magazine publishers send to authors who have submitted unsolicited manuscripts contracts that say, "This work will be a work made for hire." This is illogical and ineffective; at most, such a contract will be interpreted as a transfer of copyright ownership from the author to the magazine. On the other hand, if a work truly is commissioned, nothing says the written agreement to consider it a work for hire may not be signed after the work is done. For safety's sake, though, it probably should be signed as soon afterward as possible.

This new rule for commissioned works creates an interesting problem that may have to be solved by litigation. The problem is this: If *A* commissions *B* to create a work of some sort, and it is not a work made for hire, what rights do *A* and *B* actually have in the work? If it is a portrait, for example, *A* obviously has ownership of the portrait itself and has a limited right to display it publicly.[15] *A* does not own any other rights in it.

Suppose, though, that the work is something *A* intends to use, such as advertising material. Fairness would dictate that *A* has a nonexclusive license to publish the work, to display or perform it, and to make new versions or other derivative works based upon it. However, does *B* have to give *A* access to the plates and negatives, or master tapes, so that *A* can reproduce the work conveniently? The statute does not say. Under the old law, it was usually held that a commissioning party had the copyright and thus was entitled to the plates, negatives, and similar material.[16] The issue simply did not arise. However, under the new law, there is no such easy way out.

Would *B* be at liberty to revise the same advertising materials for the use of another client? Logically, he ought to be, but it is not at all clear that this is so.[17] This paradoxical state of affairs underlines the clear need for a written contract in all such cases.

Finally, I should point out one interesting and potentially important twist in the law governing those special categories of commissioned works. The statute permits them to be considered works made for hire only if they are "specially ordered or commissioned for use as" a contribution to a collective work, a translation, or whatever. What if the commissioned work is not used in the way originally intended? For example, suppose that a drawing is commissioned to be used as a contribution to a periodical, but the publisher decides instead to use it as an illustration for a book, that is, as a supplementary work. Will the publisher still be considered the author? The law remains untested, and the matter is pure speculation, but it is a possibility to consider. People commissioning works should specify in the contract that those works may be used in any way the commissioning party thinks appropriate.

Authorship of Compilations

The term *compilation*, as used in the copyright law, covers any kind of work that assembles facts or brings together a number of independently created works. It includes directories, dictionaries, racing forms, and the like. It also includes the vast category of works known as "collective works": magazines, anthologies, and so on. It does not include collages, poems like *The Waste*

Land, or other works where the elements are brought together in artistic fusion. The author of a compilation is the person who does the compiling. The copyright in a compilation covers the arrangement and selection of material.

Authorship of Works Created with the Aid of Computers

A computer-made work is frequently the result of human teamwork. If the members of the team are employees of a common employer, the employer will be the author of any work created, because of the work-made-for-hire doctrine. If, however, the team members come together voluntarily, can they be considered joint authors? At first it would seem so, but on close inspection this theory falls apart.

I will take up again my earlier example of a Biblical concordance. The statute defines a joint work as one "prepared by two or more authors with the intention that their contributions be merged into inseparable or interdependent parts of a unitary whole." Suppose Smith, Jones, and Brown enter into an agreement to write a concordance, with Smith taking charge of developing the program, Jones compiling the data base, and Brown "inputting" the program and processing the data. There would seem to be no question but that all three are joint authors of whatever is ultimately produced. But a strict reading of the statute does not permit such an interpretation. The computer program is separate from any printout the computer makes, it remains intact, unchanged, and this is true whether we call the program in object code form a copyrightable writing or a patentable device. Thus, it would be illogical to say that the program is an "inseparable or interdependent part" of the printout, and illogical to call Smith, the author of the program, a joint author.

This reasoning may soothe those who purchase software for research purposes; it would certainly be unfair to expect them to divide their profits with the software retailer. But it wreaks havoc with enterprises such as that of Smith, Jones and Brown, and forces Smith to resort to contract, or to partnership or trust law, for protection of his rights. Nonetheless that appears to be the law, and persons finding themselves in Smith's position should seek contractual protection.[18]

These arguments apply with equal force to Jones, the creator of the data base. We have thus excluded from the team of would-be joint authors both the software designer and the data base assembler. Nor does there seem to be any way around this result, short of changing the law so that in every case the author of a computer program or data base is a joint author of the end product, a change that would have a devastating impact on the software industry.

Divisibility

The principles of authorship determine who owns copyright at the time a work is first fixed in tangible form. At that point, a property right comes into being, and may be transferred to others. At that point also, the principle of divisibility comes into play.

A copyright is in reality a bundle of rights, each of which may be exploited separately. These rights are: to reproduce the work, to distribute it to the public, to perform it publicly, to display it publicly, and to create derivative works based upon it. The author may transfer any one or more of them without transferring the others. The owner or exclusive licensee of any of these rights is, with respect to that right, a "copyright owner." He is like a tenant who can sublet to a third person and collect rent from the subtenant.

The divisibility principle goes farther than this, though, for each of these five rights can in turn be carved up in a hundred ways. A novelist need not give a publisher the entire publication right to her novel.

She may give one publisher the hardcover rights and another publisher the paperback rights. A playwright need not sell to a producer his entire performance right; he may give the stage right to one producer and the television right to another. Rights can be carved up geographically and chronologically as well. There is no end, in fact, to the number of possible subsidiary rights, although some of them are more appropriate to some kind of works than to others. And any of those licensees, such as the television producer, is considered an owner of the work, to the extent of his license, so long as the license is exclusive.[19]

It is important to remember that copyright in a work is separate from the physical object. The person who owns a work of art, for example, does not necessarily own copyright in it.[20] All he owns is the right to display it publicly, and even that right does not extend to display by means of television broadcast. Furthermore, if the object is a movie or other audiovisual work, he can display only one frame at a time.[21]

This means that the author of a work retains copyright even if the work itself is sold or given away. There is one major gap in this rule, however. Although the author theoretically owns the right to copy the work, nothing in the law requires the owner to give the author access to the actual object. An artist who has sold a canvas may find the right to copy it a rather empty privilege.

Community Property

A special problem of ownership affects those who live in states that treat property acquired during marriage as belonging equally to husband and wife. Is a copyright acquired after a marriage subject to this so-called "community property" rule? No one really knows. No case has ever been decided on the point. I think it likely that the answer under the new statute is "no"; the new statute appears to override any state laws that might otherwise regulate copyright ownership. Arguably the same was true even under the old statute, at least as to published works. But in the absence of a judicial pronouncement, all this is conjecture.

Duration of Copyright

Authorship determines not only ownership of a copyright, but also its duration. The regular term is life of the author plus fifty years. In the case of a joint work, though, it is life of the last joint author to die plus fifty years. In either case, the copyright runs until the end of the calendar year fifty years after the author's death.

Suppose you do not know if or when an author might have died. Does the copyright go on and on forever, sheltered by public ignorance? No; the law provides that if, seventy-five years after first publication of a work or one hundred years after its creation, the records of the Copyright Office contain no information as to the author's being alive, or as to when the author died, the author will be presumed to have been dead for fifty years. Anyone who does not have reason to know that this is wrong can act on this presumption without being regarded as an infringer. The only requirement is that he must obtain from the Copyright Office a certified report that it has no information on the subject. Whether he will be able to continue using the work once he learns the author has not been dead for fifty years is unclear at this point.

This situation can be avoided. The law provides that anyone who has a stake in the copyright can file a statement with the Copyright Office, indicating that the author is still alive, or that he died on such-and-such a date. This may or may not be desirable, of course; it would actually shorten the copyright term if the author dies fewer than twenty-five years after publication of the work or, in some cases, fewer than fifty years after its creation.

There are exceptions to the "life plus fifty" rule. The most common is that of a work made for hire. Copyright in a work made for hire lasts for seventy-five years from the date of first publication or one hundred years from the date of creation, whichever is the shorter period. Suppose, for example, that in 1978 a publisher of a children's story commissioned someone to illustrate it as a work for hire, and the story, complete with illustrations, was published in 1979. The writer has a copyright in the story for her lifetime plus fifty years, but copyright in the illustrations, which are made for hire, lasts for seventy-five years (that is, through December 31, 2054). However, if the book is not published until 2012, copyright in the illustrations would expire in 2079 (one hundred years from the date of creation) rather than in 2087 (seventy-five years from the date of publication). These provisions also apply to any joint work if any contribution to it is made for hire.[22] Thus, if the story and illustrations I have just described were considered parts of a joint work, the work-for-hire duration rules would govern.

The term for a work that is authored anonymously or under a pseudonym is much the same as for a work made for hire. If the records of the Copyright Office contain no information as to the true identity of the author, the copyright term, like that of a work made for hire, will be seventy-five years from first publication or one hundred years from creation, whichever period expires first.

At any time up to the expiration of this period, anyone who has a stake in the copyright can file a statement in the Copyright Office revealing the identity of the author.[23] As of that moment, the copyright term becomes life plus fifty years (unless, of course, the work is also a work made for hire). This may not be desirable; if the author died, say, five years after publishing the work, revealing the author's identity will actually cause the copyright term to be shorter than it would have been if he had remained incognito. This situation creates an opportunity for the unscrupulous. Suppose that a movie producer owns the movie rights to a novel written under a pseudonym, and has made a film that still, fifty years after the author's death, continues to produce yearly revenues. A rival film company, by buying up some other right in the novel, could obtain a stake in the copyright and be entitled to file a statement revealing the author's identity. The work would then be in the public domain, and the rival would be able to make a film of his own.

There is no way to protect yourself against this situation. However, if you are publishing a work under a pseudonym, you should require in every contract by which you transfer any interest in your copyright that the purchaser promises not to reveal your identity unless doing so will lengthen your copyright term. You should also require every purchaser to make the same demand of everyone purchasing from him. In this way you will preserve a right to sue for damages if a statement is filed to your detriment.

3

Transfers of Copyright

An argument can be made that the word *property* never refers to an actual object, but only to the right to use or dispose of it. It is this, I think, that underlies our use of the word *property* for so intangible a possession as copyright.

Because copyright is property, it can be sold, given away, donated to charity, bequeathed by will, or rented out on whatever terms the owner desires. And the same is true of any subsidiary right, such as the right to publish, the right to perform, and so on. However, copyright differs from most other kinds of property in two important respects.

First, the property of individual authors (as opposed to corporations that are authors of works made for hire) is immunized in an unusual way from government interference. Until an individual author has made at least one exclusive license or grant of his copyright, or some part of it—for example, the right to perform the work publicly—no part of his copyright can be expropriated, transferred, or confiscated from the author by any court or other governmental body for any purpose or any reason (including, presumably, nonpayment of taxes).[1]

Second, a sale or other transfer that appears to be absolute and irrevocable may be revoked (or "terminated", to use the language of the statute) by the author or by his heirs, provided that certain procedures are followed. This is a statutory right and does not affect any right of termination that the author may have reserved by contract.

Of these two special rules, the second is likely to be the most important in years to come. It was enacted to prevent a recurrence in the future of the sad tales we know so well, in which the hero signs away his copyright for a pittance only to see the villain reap enormous profits. Whether the new rule will have any practical value for the average work remains to be seen.

Making a Transfer

A transfer, often referred to as a grant, of a copyright or any right under it, can be either exclusive or non-exclusive, depending on the needs of those involved. Nonexclusive grants tend to be for limited periods of time; for example, a high school theater company needs no more than a nonexclusive license for its spring play. A book publisher, on the other hand, will insist on getting an exclusive publication right in a manuscript.

A nonexclusive license can be as informal as a handshake. An exclusive license or other exclusive transfer—be it a mortgage, sale, gift, or bequest—must be in writing and must be signed by the person making it. With regard to unpublished works, this did not use to be so. The old rule was that common law copyrights could be transferred orally or even by implication.[2]

The only instance in which an exclusive transfer does not need to be a signed instrument is where it comes about by what is called "operation of law." For example, if an author dies without a will, the law of the state where she lives will give her copyright to her heirs, and no written instrument is needed.[3]

"Exclusive" is not so narrow as it seems. You can give an exclusive license to perform a play in Alaska if you put the agreement in writing and sign it. You can give an exclusive license to perform a play for a limited period of time, say five years. You can give one person an exclusive license to distribute a work by mail and another person an exclusive license to sell over the counter.

Any limit on a license must be expressly stated.[4] If the license is in writing, the limitation should be as well; if the license is by word of mouth, the limitation must be understood by both parties.

Sometimes, though, limitations on a license are less clear than they seem. For example, writers of stories or novels frequently give movie producers something called "motion picture rights." This phrase and others like it have created a lot of litigation over whether television broadcast of the movie is permitted by the license. (The source of the contention is that television is not the traditional means or place of showing a movie.)[5] The cases have gone both ways, depending on minor differences in wording. This, and similar problems of interpretation, underline the need for careful drafting of licenses. This particular problem can be avoided by a clause something like this: "The producer will have the right to perform and display his motion picture in any manner and by any means now known or later developed."

The only clear exception to the rule that limitations on a license must be expressly stated is for contributions to collective works. Here the statute reverses the general rule. It provides that if you contribute, say, a poem to an anthology, the owner of the anthology can publish it only in that anthology, revisions of that anthology, or later works in the same series, unless you give a broader license. A contribution to a magazine would be another common example; the publisher is presumed to acquire only the right to publish it in issues of that magazine. This is a major departure from the pre-1978 law.[6]

Can a license be transferred? In other words, can a licensee give someone else part or all of his license? Here, too, the law has changed since 1977. Under the old law sublicensing, as this is called, was not allowed unless the licensee was clearly given that right.[7] Under the new law, the answer depends on whether the license is exclusive or nonexclusive. It is fairly clear under the new statute that an exclusive license can be transferred.[8] However, nothing in the new law seems to have changed the old rule with respect to nonexclusive licenses.

Drafting a Transfer Agreement

The written instrument necessary for an exclusive transfer can come in many shapes and sizes, and may be executed at any time before or after the transfer takes effect.[9] A written memorandum of the transfer will suffice, if it is signed by the transferor. A letter from an author to her mother describing the transfer could satisfy the requirement if a court found it to be adequate evidence. If you are getting a license and are afraid that someone will try to question the existence of the transfer—for example, by claiming that the author's signature is forged—have the instrument of transfer notarized.[10]

For the benefit of all concerned, any copyright transfer should clearly state, in addition to royalty provisions, warranties, and so on, the answers to the following questions:

1. What rights are being transferred? If the entire copyright, a clause often used is, "X hereby transfers to Y his entire right, title and interest, including copyright in and to a certain work entitled *Mud Wrestling for Fun and Profit*." Otherwise be quite specific; for example: "X hereby transfers to Y his entire right to

perform publicly a certain work entitled *Mud Wrestling for Fun and Profit*"; or "X hereby licenses to Y the exclusive right to make audiovisual works based upon X's work entitled *Mud Wrestling for Fun and Profit*."

2. How long is the transfer to last? What other limitations are there?

3. When, how, and for what reasons can the transfer be terminated? (If not at all, nothing needs to be said on this point.)

4. Whose name will be placed in the notice on any published copies? Every contract concerning publication should require that the person receiving the grant place proper copyright notice on all published copies.[11]

5. Who will bear the cost of prosecuting or defending any infringement suit?

6. How will damages won in any such suit be apportioned?

7. Who will pay if someone wins an infringement suit against the work?

To keep their dealings with their authors private, many publishers are limiting their instruments of transfer to a brief description of the transfer and dealing with the other issues (points 3 through 7) in a separate contract. Thus, when they record with the Copyright Office, they file only a single sheet of paper. This is a practice I recommend to anyone drafting a copyright agreement. If you follow this practice, your separate contract should state, "The instrument of transfer concerning this work is incorporated in this contract by reference and made a part of this contract." In this way, the two documents are tied together for other purposes.

Recording the Transfer The written evidence of a transfer—be it a contract, a memorandum, or a letter—may be recorded in the Copyright Office. The fee is $10 for recordation of up to six pages concerning only one work; each additional work and each page over six will incur an addition of $.50 to the fee. For example, recordation totaling eight pages and covering two works will be charged a fee of $11.50.[12]

When recordation has been completed in the Copyright Office, the person who records will receive a certificate of recordation; duplicate certificates can be obtained from the Copyright Office for $4 apiece.[13]

Recordation that clearly identifies the work will give general notice to the world at large of the facts set forth in the recorded document. Other people are presumed to have notice of all the information recorded, regardless of whether they have actually seen the document. For this is to be so, however, the work must also be registered (see chapter 5).[14] Recordation of a transfer cannot be used as a substitute for registration of the underlying work.

Two People Claiming the Same Right

One important effect of recording a transfer is to establish priority of ownership. Suppose that a novelist sells dramatization rights in his novel to Smith on April 1 and then on April 2 sells the same rights to Jones. Smith has a one-month "grace period" in which to record the transfer (two months if the transfer is executed outside the country). After that time it is a horse race: Jones will be regarded as the legal owner of the copyright if he records before Smith, even though the transfer to him took place later than that to Smith.[15]

But again, this is true only if the work has been registered. Thus we see the lengths to which Congress has been willing to go to induce people to register copyright claims. If the work is not registered, or until it is registered, no one has priority over anyone else, and neither Smith nor Jones may sue the other for going about his business. It is therefore in the interest

of anyone who is recording a transfer to ensure that
the work is registered.

There are two important circumstances under which
these rules of priority do not apply. First, if the later
transfer is a gift or bequest it cannot take precedence
over a sale that preceded it, no matter when the sale
is actually recorded.[16] This result seems only fair; it
would be hard to justify a law that gave precedence
to someone who had paid nothing for a right over
someone who had paid. Second, if the person who
received the second transfer actually knew of the first
transfer he cannot take precedence over the earlier purchaser by beating him to the Copyright Office. This,
too, seems only fair.

The question of priority occurs not only between one
transfer and another but also between a transfer of
ownership and a nonexclusive license. Suppose, for
instance, that a playwright sells performing rights in
her play to a Broadway producer and later in the week
gives permission to a local troupe to perform the same
play. If the nonexclusive license was taken by the local
troupe without knowledge of the prior transfer and
before the transfer was recorded, the troupe has the
right to perform the work within the limits of its license
without regard to the rights of the producer. This is so
regardless of whether the nonexclusive license itself is
in writing and regardless of whether it is recorded.[17]

Suppose, in another instance, that the nonexclusive
license is given before the sale of rights is made. Here,
again, the nonexclusive license takes priority over the
transfer, regardless of whether or when either of them
is recorded. The nonexclusive license in such a case is
like a right-of-way over a piece of land: any purchaser
of the land is obligated to honor the right-of-way.

In no instance does it matter whether the nonexclusive license was paid for or was a gift or bequest. In

this, the law with respect to nonexclusive licenses differs fundamentally from the law of exclusive transfers.

Recordation as a Prerequisite for Suit

However valid his ownership, no one other than the author may bring suit for infringement until he has recorded the transfer by which he obtained his copyright. (This does not apply to pre-1978 oral transfers of common law copyright.) This does not mean that the owner can sue only for infringements that occur after he records, but it does mean that to sue for past infringements he must first pay his fee and give the general public notice of his rights.[18]

How does someone who receives a copyright by bequest fit into this scheme? When the statute speaks of a transfer, it means any kind of conveyance, and a will is regarded as an instrument of conveyance.[19] Therefore, in order to receive the protection that recordation gives, a beneficiary of an author's will should record the will in the Copyright Office. He will not be able to attain priority over a transfer that was made during the author's life; however, recordation of the will gives notice of the transfer of ownership to all interested persons and may have the beneficial effect of making it more difficult for someone else claiming to own the dead author's rights to make a fraudulent sale. Of course, a beneficiary does not need to record the will until he wishes to sue someone for infringement.

Recordation of Licenses for Public Broadcasting

If you give any public broadcasting station or network a license to perform or display a published musical work or to display a published work of art, whether or not you also give it the right to tape the performance or display, you should require it to record the license within thirty days. If the license is not recorded, you will be bound by the terms of a compulsory license created by statute (see chapter 7).

Termination of Transfers   In addition to any termination right an author may reserve in a contract, the author and his heirs have a termination right under the copyright statute. This statutory right of termination, unlike the copyright itself, cannot be contracted away, given away, or bequeathed. No agreement that anyone can persuade an author to sign will diminish his right or the right of his heirs to terminate a grant of copyright.[20] For this reason, a contract clause requiring the author to pay the other party money if he exercises his termination right would probably be held invalid under the new law. In short, the right to terminate is not a property right but a privilege under the law. It extends to all works other than those made for hire and to all grants except those of rights in foreign countries.[21]

In general, only grants made by a living author, and made after December 31, 1977, may be terminated. Other grants, even those made by the author in his will, are not subject to termination.[22] An exception for certain pre-1978 works is discussed in chapter 9.

After termination, the person who once owned the right or license cannot exploit the work further in any way. There is one exception: if someone has made a derivative work under a grant permitting him to do so, he can continue to exploit this work, because the derivative work has a separate copyright. Termination prevents him only from making or authorizing further derivative works.[23]

The statutory termination right is open only to authors, their widows or widowers, and their children and grandchildren (whether legitimate or not and whether natural or adopted). Someone else who has received a right from an author, or even the entire copyright, and transferred to a third person, is not protected by the law.[24]

The right is also limited in time. Termination may be made only in a five-year period beginning thirty-five years after the date of the grant and ending forty years after the date of the grant. The only variation from this rule is in the case of a publication right. The five-year period in which a grant of a publication right may be terminated can begin at one of two times: either forty years after the date of the grant or thirty-five years after the date of first publication, whichever is earlier.[25]

Certain procedures must be followed in exercising this right. These procedures apply whether the original grant or license was exclusive or nonexclusive; even a word-of-mouth license cannot be terminated except by following the rules.[26]

If the work is a joint work and two or more of the joint authors execute a grant, termination may be made only by a majority of those authors who executed the grant. The law does not require a majority of the interest in the work, only a numerical majority of the authors who made the grant. Because nonexclusive transfers of copyright in a joint work can be made by one joint author without the others' consent, the termination rules focus on who made the grant, not who owns the copyright. In other words, even if one of three joint authors is entitled, by agreement with the others, to 60 percent of the royalties, he cannot singlehandedly terminate a grant unless he alone made it. The majority requirement also means that if only two authors executed the grant, they must both join in the termination for it to be effective.

Just what obligations one joint author has to another in this respect is unclear. Co-owners are liable to each other for profits, and in many cases for loss they may cause to the income-producing ability of what they own. Will joint authors be liable to each other for loss of revenues, if the loss is caused by termination of a grant? My guess is that they will not be, because the termination is a legal right created by statute.

If an author or a joint author is dead, his right to terminate or to join in a termination may be exercised by his surviving spouse (regardless of remarriage) and his children or grandchildren. The spouse controls half of the right and the children or grandchildren the other half. If there are no children or grandchildren the spouse controls the entire right, and if there is no spouse the children and grandchildren control the entire right. The statute makes no provision for an author being survived only by great-grandchildren. It is not clear why great-grandchildren were given no rights under the statute, but that is the case.

If children or grandchildren own the termination right, or one-half of it, what they own is to be divided among them in equal shares. This division into shares is a *per stirpes* distribution. This means that if, for example, an author's daughter is dead but has surviving children, her share belongs to her children and may be exercised only by a majority of them. If all of an author's children are dead, the surviving grandchildren do not take equally; each set of grandchildren takes the share that would belong to their parent if he or she were alive.

The required percentage: The termination right of a deceased author may be exercised only by persons owning, among them, over 50 percent of the termination right. For example, if there are a widow, one child, and three grandchildren of a deceased child, the widow owns 50 percent of the right, the child owns 25 percent, and the three grandchildren among them own 25 percent, but can exercise their 25 percent only if a majority of them agree. In such a case, termination can take place only if the child or two of the grandchildren agree to terminate. If there are a widower, one child, and two grandchildren, either the child or both grandchildren must join with the widower. If there is no spouse but there are three children, two of the children must join together.

Notice of termination must be given in advance. This notice must be in writing and must be signed by the necessary persons or their authorized agents. It must specify the exact date on which termination is to become effective. That date must be within the appropriate five-year period. Notice itself must be given at least two years before that date, but not more than ten years before it. Notice must be recorded (for a $10 fee) in the Copyright Office before that date, or it will be invalid. The notice must be served, in hand or by first-class mail, on "the grantee or the grantee's successor in title," that is, on the person who originally received the transfer, or on anyone who has obtained it from him.

This language is anything but self-explanatory. Suppose the grantee (the person who received the transfer) has sold it to someone else without your knowledge. If you serve notice only on the grantee, will that terminate the rights of the person he sold it to? If we say "yes," we are perhaps creating hardship for the second purchaser. If we say "no," we are perhaps creating hardship for you, the author.

Neither the statute nor the regulations of the Copyright Office shed much light on this problem. It will be one for the courts to clarify. My guess—or more accurately, my hope—is that the terminator will be held only to his own personal knowledge of what subsequent transfers have been made and to a knowledge of any transfers recorded in the Copyright Office. If the author is a composer whose work is handled by ASCAP or one of the other performing rights societies, he will also have a duty to check the society's records. If his search reveals no "successor in title," it will be

enough that he has served notice on the original grantee. This puts the burden on the successors in title to
record the instruments by which they obtain their
rights, and that seems not only a fair allocation of the
burden but one in keeping with the law's general policy
of encouraging recordation.

**Copyright
after
Termination**

As of the date that notice of termination is served, the
right or rights that are to terminate become vested in
the persons who own the termination right.[27] For example, as of the date that a playwright's widow and
children terminate his grant of the performance rights,
the performance right vests in them. Vesting means
entitlement, not actual possession; what happens is
that the rights that will eventually revert, when the
termination takes effect, are allocated before that time,
and are a limited kind of property interest.

The rights vest in everyone who could have joined
in the termination, regardless of whether he actually
did take part in it. If, for example, an author's son did
not take part in giving notice of termination, he will
still get his proportionate share of the right when it
reverts. If the termination is made by the family of a
deceased author, the rights vest in the same *per stirpes*
manner described earlier. In the case of a joint work,
nothing vests in an author (or the family of an author)
who did not join in the original grant, since he did not
own a termination right with respect to that grant.

**Making a New
Transfer**

Because vesting is less than actual possession, the rule
that the rights vest as of the date notice is received
does not mean that the new owners can make a new
transfer immediately. They cannot make a new grant
of any kind, exclusive or nonexclusive, before the date
of termination; not even the author can do this. Moreover, with one exception, the owner or owners in whom

the right vests cannot even make an agreement to make a grant before the date of termination. And because selling the right to make a grant is tantamount to making a grant, it is probable that even someone who receives the entire right, when that right vests, cannot sell his right to make a new grant until the date that termination takes effect.

The exception to this rule is that the people terminating may renegotiate a contract with the existing right holder.[28] For example, if a publisher has a license to make and sell reproductions of a photograph, the photographer or her appropriate heirs can give notice of termination and immediately thereafter renegotiate the contract. The renegotiated royalties do not, theoretically, take effect until the date that termination actually occurs, but if the license is a lucrative one, the publisher may well compromise on this point, and pay more royalties in the interim in order to get a renewal of the grant.

It is important to remember that the right to terminate inheres in the person; it is less like property than like a privilege. It cannot be sold or given away. If an author's widow dies, the termination right that she possessed dies with her, and the entire termination right belongs to the children or grandchildren, if any. If they in turn die and leave no descendants of their own, the whole privilege comes to an end, and the license or transfer will continue on for the rest of the copyright term, immune from termination. However, once notice of termination is given and reversion of the copyright becomes vested in the people who had a right to terminate, we are talking not of a privilege but once again of a property right.

Unlike the right to terminate, this property right does not die with the owner; he can bequeath it in his will to anyone at all, and whoever receives the bequest can take part in any renegotiations or new grants. Presumably, also, the owner can sell or give away his right to receive income from his share of the copyright. But unless he owns the entire copyright, he cannot sell or give away during his life his right to take part in making a new grant because the law makes very stringent requirements for new grants of terminated rights.

Mechanics of Making a New Transfer

A renegotiation, or a new grant, must be made in the following manner:[29]

1. It must be in writing. This requirement applies not only to transfers but also to nonexclusive licenses. (This is the only circumstance in which a nonexclusive license is required to be in writing.)

2. It must be signed by persons representing at least the same proportion of ownership in the right as was involved in the termination.

3. It must be signed by the same number of persons as signed the notice of termination.

These requirements concerning number and proportion are difficult to grasp. It may be helpful to take an example. Suppose that an author dies, survived by a wife, one daughter, and two grandsons born of a deceased son. Because termination of the original grant requires participation of over 50 percent of the termination right, in this case it will require 75 percent of the right—the widow's 50 percent, plus another 25 percent: either the living daughter or the deceased son as represented by his children. It will also require at least two signatures.

When the right vests in the author's family, upon the giving of notice of termination, it vests 50 percent in the widow, 25 percent in the daughter, and $12\frac{1}{2}$ percent in each of the two grandsons. (Each of these people now owns a separate and distinct interest because the rights are vested.) Suppose the widow then dies, bequeathing her entire share of the right to one of the grandsons, so that he now owns $62 1/2$ percent of the right. The law provides that someone who inherits an interest in a right in this way "represents" the person from whom he received it, for purposes of signing a new grant. Thus the grandson represents his grandmother, and he may sign the new grant on behalf of his grandmother as well as on his own behalf, so that, in effect, there are two signatures on the document. This meets the "number" requirement, since there were only two signatures on the notice of termination. However, despite the fact that he now owns over half the right, the grandson cannot singlehandedly make a new grant, for the new grant must be agreed to by 75 percent of the ownership—that being the percentage of the ownership which agreed to the termination. Therefore, to make a new grant, this grandson must persuade either his brother or his aunt to join him. If he cannot, no new grant can be made.

Once a new grant or a renegotiation of an old grant has been made, it binds and benefits everyone who had a share of the right to make it, regardless of whether he actually signs the new grant or renegotiation.[30] In the previous example, if only the widow and the two grandsons join in making the new grant, the daughter is nonetheless treated as if she too had joined in. By "binds" I mean that when the new grant is made she cannot make a grant of any kind on her own; on the other hand, she is entitled to her share of the proceeds. To take another example, if an author's husband and one of her two children terminate an old grant and then renegotiate it or make a new grant to someone else, the other child cannot go off on his own and arrange a separate sale, but on the other hand, he is entitled to a 25 percent share of the profits that the rest of the family have negotiated.

4

Just as much as copyright is property, it is also a bundle of procedures, paperwork, and footwork. All these must be followed scrupulously in order to protect a copyright.

Common law copyright is acquired upon creation of a work and lost upon fixation of it in tangible form. For purposes of the federal statute, you acquire copyright upon fixation of the work, and at any point prior to completed fixation, you automatically have copyright in as much of the work as you have fixed. As long as the work is not published, the copyright runs undisturbed until the end of the term set by the statute. Once the work is published, however, you forfeit the copyright if you do not affix notice of copyright to it.

Publication   The concept of publication is crucial to copyright law. Publication is the act of offering copies to the public. There does not have to be an actual distribution.[1] Even if there is a distribution, it does not have to be a sale; giving copies away to the public is sufficient. The size of the public is irrelevant; handing out one or two copies can constitute publication.[2] And though performance or display of a work is not publication in and of itself, distributing copies to a group of persons who will themselves perform or display the work does count as publication, unless those persons are your employees or otherwise acting under your control.[3]

The sale of one's painting, sculpture, or other work of visual art probably constitutes a publication in the eyes of the law, although there is some evidence that Congress did not intend this result.[4] But this is not a cause for great concern, because the rules of copyright notice do not require that a notice be placed on the original of an art work if no other copies are produced.

Performance and display of a work do not constitute publication. You can perform or display a work as often as you like, to as wide an audience as you like, and you will not be considered to have published it by doing so. (Both "performance" and "display" include broadcasting, film projection, and so on.)[5] Delivering a speech does not publish it.

Nor does circulation of copies within a limited group, for limited purposes, count as publication. However, the persons receiving those copies must understand that they have no right to perform or display them publicly or to make a further distribution outside the group.[6] Nor is the filing of copies or phonorecords with a court or other public authority a publication.[7]

Submission of a manuscript to a publisher is a classic example of "limited publication," as it is called, for which copyright notice is not required and would, indeed, be inappropriate. In the academic community there is also a custom of circulating so-called preprints (manuscript copies of forthcoming journal articles) among colleagues for comment and discussion. This too would be a limited publication in most cases. But if you are making what you intend as a limited publication to someone who might otherwise assume he was at liberty to do with his copy whatever he likes, you would be well advised to place on the copy a legend to this effect: "This copy is for private circulation only and may not be used in any other manner."

A friend of mine in the profession once told me that at cocktail parties—those wonderful clearing houses of free legal advice—the question he is most often asked is, who owns copyright in letters. Why does this question seem to trouble so many apparently respectable citizens? Whatever the reason, the answer will comfort them, for it is the writer who owns copyright unless there is some clear indication to the contrary. However, the recipient would have the right to make the letter public if it were necessary for some reason—perhaps to his defense against a libel action, or to clearing his character, or something of that sort.[8]

When is Notice Required?

In the case of copies from which a work can be "perceived visually," copyright notice must be placed on all copies publicly distributed, whether in the United States or elsewhere. It is not necessary that visual perception be possible with the naked eye; it is enough that the copy distributed can be perceived visually with the aid of a machine or device, such as a movie projector. Also, musical works are regarded as being visually perceived when they are written in sheet-music notation, and the same theory applies to notation of choreography.

Sound recordings are works that by definition cannot be perceived visually. They are not distributed in the form of "copies" but in the form of "phonorecords." The term *phonorecord* is a hybrid word adopted by the new law. It includes records, tapes, player-piano rolls, and any other method now known or discovered in the future for fixing sounds, but it does not include the soundtracks of audiovisual works.[9] Every phonorecord that is distributed to the public must bear notice of copyright with respect to the sound recording that it embodies. However, no notice of copyright in the underlying work need be affixed to the phonorecord.

A new and interesting question, which no court has yet faced, concerns the computer programs that embody so-called "computer music." These programs are written to drive the synthesizers that both imitate (or embellish) sounds of more traditional instruments and create entirely new sounds of their own. By the time they enter the synthesizers (which are computers connected to sound-producing mechanisms), they are in disk, tape, or other object code form. Is such a tape or disk a phonorecord of a sound recording, or a copy of a musical work? Like any more conventional phonorecord its primary function is to cause a machine to produce sound. On the other hand, the program begins life as a series of written notations, which can be likened to the notes on sheet music, and hence constitute a "copy." Under current doctrine an object code version of a source code program is a copy of it, not a derivative work. Thus, by an equally logical train of thought, we can conclude that the disk or tape is a copy of the musical work, not a phonorecord.

For now, this conundrum is merely intriguing. But the day is probably not far off when there will be a market for computer music among a large segment of the public who can afford to own synthesizers, and floppy disks of computer music will occupy a corner of every music store. What kind of copyright symbol will those floppy disks bear—℗ or ©? (For the moment you'd be wise to affix both.) How should the source codes be registered—as musical works or as sound recordings? Will it be possible to acquire a compulsory license (see chapter 7) to make other floppy disks of the same music? If so, what will be the scope of the license? It seems that fewer problems will arise if we consider the disk to be a copy of the underlying musical notation, but I would hesitate to predict that this will in fact be the rule.

Notice for Contributions to a Collective Work

One question frequently asked is, What notice is needed on a magazine article, or a poem in an anthology, or any other contribution to a collective work? All contributions to a collective work are protected by a general notice affixed to the collective work as a whole, except for advertisements, which must bear separate notice or risk going into the public domain.[10] However, if the contributor retains copyright, omission of separate notice may be treated as if notice had been given in the wrong name. See *Mistake in Name* below. Therefore it is a good idea to require, if you can, that your contribution to a collective work have its own copyright notice.

Formalities of Copyright Notice

Notice comprises three things:

1. In the case of visually perceived works, the familiar symbol ©, or, if you prefer, the word "Copyright" or its accepted abbreviation, "Copr." (If you wish to be certain that your work is protected in foreign countries, use ©; the word *Copyright* and the abbreviation *Copr.* do not have international validity.) In the case of sound recordings published in phonorecords, the only symbol to use is ℗; © is of no effect.[11]

2. The year of first publication. This date is necessary except where a visual work is reproduced in or on greeting cards, postcards, stationery, jewelry, dolls, toys, or "useful articles" (articles having an intrinsic utilitarian function).[12] A good example of this useful-article exception would be the reproduction of a painting on a placemat; in such a case, the date when the painting itself was first published would not need to be included in the copyright notice.

Bear in mind that the year of first publication of a work may not necessarily be the year in which you are first required to affix copyright notice. For example, a musical work is considered to be "published" by the distribution of phonorecords or movie soundtracks embodying it, even though those phonorecords and soundtracks do not need to bear notice as to the musical work. Thus, if a piece of music comes out on a record in 1984 but not in sheet music form till 1986, 1984 is the proper year to put in the notice.

3. The name of the owner of copyright. This may be abbreviated if the name remains recognizable. If the owner has a generally known trademark, abbreviation, or other symbol, that symbol may be used instead. This term *owner of copyright* is different from the term *copyright owner* (who may be merely the owner of the exclusive publication right). The owner of copyright is the author or anyone else to whom the author has transferred the entire copyright, or the bulk of copyright.[13] In the case of the sound recording, notice must be in the name of the owner of the copyright in the recording; the name of the owner of copyright in the musical composition should not be used and may lead to substantial confusion.

There is an additional requirement in the case of works that consist preponderantly of works of the U.S. Government. For example, a collection of public documents edited by a private citizen must include in the notice a statement identifying those parts of the work which are the author's and in which copyright is therefore claimed, or identifying those parts of the work which are the product of the U.S. Government, and in which copyright is therefore not claimed.

The elements of notice need not appear all together, so long as they are all present on the copy and placed in such a way that a reasonable person would understand them to be parts of a whole.

The location of the notice as a whole is important, although the law's requirements are not so strict now as they used to be. In the case of sound recordings, notice must be placed on the surface of the phonorecord, on the label, or on the container in which the phonorecord is retailed. Its placement must be calculated to give "reasonable notice" to the public.[14] In the case of visually perceived works, the only requirement is that placement be calculated to give reasonable notice to the public. Notice has to be fixed to the copy or phonorecord; the law will not be satisfied by, say, tying to a sculpture a tag with copyright notice written on it unless no alternative is feasible. The regulations of the Copyright Office, giving examples of acceptable placement of notice, are reproduced in appendix A.

As additional protection, it is advisable to place in your notice the statement, "All Rights Reserved," to ensure protection in certain Latin American countries that do not recognize "Copyright," "Copr.," or © as proper notice of a claim of rights.

Consequences of Defective Notice

What happens if the information contained in the notice is erroneous? The answer depends on whether the copies or phonorecords bearing defective notice were distributed with the copyright owner's permission. Anyone signing a contract with a publisher should make sure that it requires the publisher to place correct notice on the copies or phonorecords. This will save the author from any oversight on the publisher's part. Otherwise a court might assume that the faulty publication was made with the author's consent. Defective notice on unauthorized copies or phonorecords—for example, albums distributed by a record pirate—or in copies or phonorecords distributed in violation of the terms of the contract does not affect the rights of the copyright owner at all.

On the other hand, the law has a valid interest in making copyright owners responsible for seeing that copies or phonorecords distributed with their permission bear correct notice. The consequences of a mistake differ depending on the nature of the error. (I am speaking here of unwitting errors. Fraudulent misrepresentations in a copyright notice can bring a fine of up to $2,500.[15])

Mistake in Name

If the person whose name appears in the notice is not the real "owner of copyright"—for example, if a book bearing notice in the name of John Adams is actually the work of his wife Abigail, or if a publisher who has only the publication right puts its own name on the notice, or if a contribution to a collective work does not bear a separate copyright notice—the copyright is not lost, because the public is put on notice that somebody claims copyright in the work. What if someone in good faith purchases rights in the work from the person named in the notice and proceeds to exploit them? The law states that the purchaser will not be liable for infringement if he "begins his undertaking" before the work has been registered in the correct name or before some other document has been recorded with the Copyright Office, signed by the person whose name appears in the notice but revealing the true owner of copyright.[16] This does not mean that the good-faith purchaser actually gets a right in the work. He does not; what he gets is a sort of limited privilege to exploit the right he believed he was buying.

Fairness requires such a result. If the law were otherwise, many unlucky purchasers would find themselves with no way to recoup their investment. However, since fairness is the guiding principle, no one can say in advance how a court will decide a particular case.

The law provides that the limited privilege does not exist until the purchaser "begins his undertaking." Clearly these words mean more than the mere act of purchasing the right because at that stage the whole problem could be corrected simply by undoing the sale. Only an investment of time and resources in actually exploiting the right will tip the scales in the purchaser's favor. Will setting type be enough? Will hiring extra personnel? As to that, no one knows, for this is a new provision, and the law has not been tested.

And what is the extent of the limited privilege that the purchaser thus obtains? I believe that if he has sunk money into a big Broadway production in reliance on his bogus right, he will be permitted to exploit his bogus right at least until he has recovered his investment, perhaps even until he has made a reasonable profit. After that, does his privilege end? Again, the law is silent.

Looked at from the perspective of the copyright owner whose rights are infringed, the situation is no less shot through with ambiguity. The law provides that he is entitled to receive the profits of the person who sold the bogus right. Suppose the seller has inadvertently sold the rights for a fraction of their true worth? Can the true owner sue anybody for the difference? Probably, but no one knows for certain.

Mistake in Date   If the date written in the notice is earlier than the true date of first publication, in the ordinary case there will be no repercussions. But if the work is published anonymously or under a pseudonym or is a work made for hire, so that the copyright term is computed with reference to the first date of publication, the term will be computed from the date given in the notice, and the copyright owner will lose a year or more of protection.

If the date given in the notice is later than the date of first publication by only a year, there will be no repercussions, except that in the case of a work published anonymously or under a pseudonym or in the case of a work made for hire, the date given in the notice will be ignored, and the copyright term will be computed using the correct date.

If the date in the notice is two or more years later than the actual date of first publication, then the work will be treated as if the date had been omitted altogether.[17]

Omission of Notice

If any one of the three principal components of proper notice—name, date, and the symbol, word, or abbreviation for "copyright"—is omitted, the work will be treated as if notice were omitted entirely.[18] Where the work consists preponderantly of U.S. Government works and the notice does not say so, the work will be treated as if notice were omitted entirely.[19]

Omission of notice destroys copyright, and the work goes into the public domain. This will not be true, however, in these cases:

• The omission was in violation of an express understanding between the copyright owner and whoever was responsible for publication. (This underscores again the importance of stating in your contract with a publisher, or any other person to whom you make a transfer of publication rights, that he has a duty to put proper notice on every copy.)

• The notice is omitted from only a relatively small number of copies that were distributed to the public.

• The application for registration, complete with fee and the necessary number of copies, is filed before the date of the publication from which notice is omitted.

• The complete application for registration is filed within five years after first publication, and a "reasonable effort" is made to add notice to all copies that have been distributed to the public, within the United States, since the omission was discovered.

A few comments on these exceptions are in order. No one knows what a "relatively small number of copies" is. Twenty thousand copies of a book with a printing of one hundred thousand is the same percent as one bronze casting out of a limited edition of five, yet the latter would be acceptable and the former probably not. "Relatively," in other words, has only the vaguest of meanings. This is another instance where the law will look to what is fair and just in a particular situation.[20]

The mass-production techniques used in modern publishing and the modern record industry make it unlikely that notice will be omitted from a relatively small number of copies or phonorecords. The difficult problems probably will arise in cases involving works reproduced by hand. A painting does not need to bear copyright notice when the painter sells it; a unique canvas comes within the exception we are discussing here. But a lithograph in an edition of two hundred is a different story. If the artist omits notice from, say, forty copies, and fails to register his copyright, and fails to make a reasonable effort to correct the omission, and if a purchaser of one of the forty copies relies on the absence of notice and starts reproducing the work himself, the artist might be out of luck. If the court decides that 40 is a relatively large number of copies in an edition of 200, the work will have entered into the public domain—and copyright, once lost, can never be regained.

No one knows what is a "reasonable effort" to correct an omission. Obviously many publishers and record companies would have great difficulty in recalling copies that had already gone out to retailers. "Reasonable effort" will probably be another matter for ad hoc determination. What happens to an author who has failed to stipulate in his publishing contract that the publisher will be responsible for proper notice? If the publisher's effort to correct notice is later found not to have been reasonable, the author, though practically powerless to correct the fault, may have lost his copyright. Can he sue the publisher? That remains to be seen.

The total effect of these rules is to make it virtually impossible at any given moment to know whether a work that lacks copyright notice is in the public domain or not. The matter is further complicated by the rule that forfeiture of copyright in a derivative work does not affect copyright in the original, so long as the forfeiture was not sanctioned by the copyright owner of the original.[21] It may be that in trying to avoid the harshness of the old rules governing notice, Congress has bent over too far backward. An item that crossed my desk several years ago is a good example. It was a newsletter published by the Bureau of National Affairs on a certain tax law being considered by Congress. The only notice on it read, "Published by Bureau of National Affairs. Right of reproduction and redistribution reserved." This clearly is not copyright notice, for it has no © and no date. It does not even tell who the copyright owner is, only who the publisher is. And yet it makes a claim to reserve publication rights. (It does not even make a claim to reserve display or derivative work rights.) It is also defective in that it does not clearly state what parts of the newsletter are U.S. Government works and not subject to copyright. Now it may be that BNA will take or has taken one of the steps permitted by law to nullify its errors. At the time, however, there was no way of knowing what one was allowed to do with this highly topical publication. Whatever arguments may favor leniency toward artists who are not copyright aficionados, nothing ought to excuse this sort of slipshod practice on the part of a company whose business is legal publishing. Perhaps the courts will exercise some discretion in this kind of case and bear down on people who are negligent to this degree, but at this point no one can tell.

The Innocent Infringer

Even if the omission of notice is excused for any of the reasons listed, the copyright owner may still suffer somewhat for his negligence if someone relies in good faith on the absence of copyright notice and proceeds to publish his own copies of the work.[22] There may be a limit to this principle. The statute exempts the infringer from liability only if he was "misled" by the absence of notice. This seems to indicate that if he has reason to believe the work actually is copyrighted, he is under a duty to investigate. If a work that is obviously original lacks copyright notice, one's first instinct would be to suspect that this omission was an error. Can one who has such a suspicion still be "misled"? At the moment, no one knows.

Although this second publisher is, technically speaking, infringing the copyright, he is protected by law from some of the penalties of infringement. For example, until it is actually brought to his notice that the work is registered with the Copyright Office, he can continue to publish without fear that he will be liable for damages. He may or may not be required to surrender his profits; that rests with the discretion of the judge or jury that hears the case; but if the negligence that led to the omission was particularly blatant, the judge or jury would be inclined to favor the infringer. Furthermore, this infringer may or may not be required by the court to stop publication, or if permitted to continue, may or may not be required to pay royalties to the copyright owner. Under no circumstances will he be required to compensate the copyright owner for damages. Damages in this context would include injury to an artist's reputation due to the circulation of poor copies of his work; it would also, presumably, include the harm that would inevitably result from the fact that the copies or phonorecords distributed by the infringer bear no copyright notice. In light of these problems, it is clear that registration is an important safety measure.

Notice on Confidential Materials

One question often asked by people in business is, what sort of copyright notice should they place on materials that contain trade secrets—know-how, customer lists, business methods, and so on? It is not an easy question to answer. The copyright law clearly states that the date contained in any copyright notice must be the year in which the work was first published, that is, first made available to members of the general public. Thus, logically, if you see a notice on a work, you are entitled to believe that the work was published in the year stated. Having been published, of course, it can no longer be secret.

Businesses are thus reluctant to put notice on confidential materials they disclose to customers, licensees, and so on. However, they ask, what happens if our disclosure is later held to have been a general publication and not a limited one? Will the absence of notice throw the material into the public domain? In response to this perceived dilemma, they sometimes put both a copyright notice and a confidentiality notice on the materials. This is hardly logical, but it has been endorsed by at least one court.[23]

There is a real risk that future courts will not concur, but will take the presence of copyright notice as evidence that a publication has in fact occurred, and that the confidentiality notice is only a self-serving statement.

My own feeling is that the perceived dilemma does not really exist. Those who obtain copies of a work on a confidential basis are, presumably, forbidden to disseminate the materials or even reproduce them except in specified circumstances. No distribution under these circumstances should be regarded as more than a limited publication.[24] Nor do we need be concerned about what happens if by accident copies bearing no notice fall into the wrong hands, for any such "publication" would be without authority of the copyright owner, and omission of notice would thus have no effect.

Legislation and regulations are under consideration that may establish some new rules for these matters. In the meantime, my suggestion is that you place a legend to the following effect on copies you distribute on a confidential basis:

The within material is an unpublished copyrighted work containing trade secret and other proprietary information of XYZ Corporation. This copy has been provided on the basis of strict confidentiality and on the express understanding that it may not be reproduced, or revealed to any person, in whole or in part, without express written permission from XYZ, which is the sole owner of copyright and all other rights therein.

By such a legend you will put all parties on notice of your copyright without running the risk that a statutory notice might be interpreted against you.

5 Registration of a Copyright Claim

Registration does not affect the existence or validity of a copyright. It is, however, important as a method of protecting one's rights under the copyright, for these reasons:

1. It can be of crucial importance if for any reason notice of copyright is accidentally omitted from copies of the work that are distributed to the public.

2. It is a prerequisite for bringing suit to enforce a copyright. (If you have attempted to register in the proper manner, but the Copyright Office has rejected your application for any reason, you may still file suit for infringement but you must give the Copyright Office notice of your suit.[1])

3. You cannot get an award of attorneys' fees or of so-called statutory damages for any infringement that takes place before the "effective date" of registration. (The effective date of registration is the date on which the application, fee, and deposit were filed, regardless of when they were finally processed.) Registration, in other words, creates the right to receive these special compensations. In the case of a published work, there is a three-month grace period for registration. If you apply for registration within three months of first publication, you can collect attorneys' fees and statutory

damages for any infringement that takes place after publication. However, there is no three-month grace period for unpublished works except films first fixed when broadcast.[2]

4. If you are the owner of copyright in a musical work, you are not entitled to royalties under a so-called compulsory license until your identity is a matter of record with the Copyright office. In practical terms, this makes registration a prerequisite to receipt of those royalties. There is no three-month grace period here.

Who May Register?

Anyone who owns or has an exclusive license for any of the rights comprised in the copyright of the work may register the work. It is the work that is being registered, not any of the subsidiary rights that make up the copyright. Registration is of the basic underlying claim in the original work.

How Is Registration Accomplished?

An application for registration has three components: the registration form, the filing fee, and deposit of copies of the work.

The Form

The registration form used will vary depending on the type of work being registered. For a nondramatic literary work other than a periodical or serial work, use form TX; for a periodical or serial work, use form SE; for a dramatic work or any other work of the performing arts (including music, dance, and film, among others), use form PA, unless you also own copyright in the sound recording of the work and are simultaneously registering your sound recording copyright, in which case you should use form SR; for a work of the visual arts (not including film or other audiovisual works), use form VA; for a sound recording, use form SR. These forms do not vary much in content, but each requests information that is especially important to the type of work it covers. These forms are available from the Information and Publications Section, Copyright Office, Library of Congress, Washington, D.C. 20559, or can be ordered by telephone at (202)287–9100.

All of the forms require certain basic information.[3]

1. The name and address of the copyright claimant. An owner of any subsidiary right under the copyright is not a "copyright claimant"; that term is used only for the author or for someone who has acquired the basic, underlying claim from the author by sale, gift, or inheritance.

2. The name of the author(s), unless the work is published anonymously or under a pseudonym.

3. The nationality or domicile of the author(s), even if the work is published anonymously or under a pseudonym.

4. If one or more of the authors is dead, the dates of their deaths.

5. If the copyright claimant is someone other than the author(s), a brief statement of how the claimant came by the copyright.

6. If the work is a compilation, a statement identifying the preexisting work or works that it incorporates; if it is a derivative work, a statement identifying the work or works on which it is based. These statements should also identify in a general way what material is original with the claimant, since that is all that is covered by the claimant's copyright.

7. A statement that the work was made for hire, if it was so.

8. The title of the work, and if in its finished state it had any other titles by which it might be identified, those others titles as well. This is particularly important if the work has been published before under a different title, a not infrequent occurrence in the case of books that were first published outside the country. The word

identified refers to identification by the public; you need not include titles by which the work has been known only to the author or private viewers. In general, if the work you are registering contains material that appeared in a different form under a different title, you would be well advised to make note of this fact when registering.

9. The year in which "creation of the work was completed"—that is, the year in which it was fixed in its final form, disregarding minor editorial changes. Remember that different versions of the work, if they differ substantially, are considered to be separate and distinct works; you should mention earlier versions of this type not under this heading but in the space where you are asked if the work is a derivative work.

10. If the work has been published, the date of its first publication and the nation in which that first publication took place.

In addition, the form for nondramatic literary works requires that you state the names of the typesetters, platemakers, printers or binders in the United States or Canada who have participated in the manufacture of the copies. This requirement reflects a provision of the law that forbids large-scale importation of copies manufactured outside the United States and Canada, if the work is authored by a United States citizen who has been living in the United States. (This provision is due to be phased out on July 1, 1986.)[4]

In any of these categories do not omit any information that may bear on the validity of the copyright claim. If you do so unintentionally, you may suffer much in lost time and money. If you do so intentionally, you run the risk of being fined up to $2,500.[5]

To illustrate how a registration form should be filled out, I have included a sample completed Form TX as appendix B at the end of this book.

The Fee

The application form must be accompanied by a $10 fee, unless the registration is of a claim for a renewal of a copyright in a work published before January 1, 1978, as to which see chapter 9.[6]

Deposit

The application must be accompanied by deposit of either one or two copies of the work, or, in special cases, some other kind of material that will identify the work you are registering.

The rules governing deposit are quite complicated. First of all, although deposit is always made with the Copyright Office, it is intended not only for the purpose of registration but also for the archival purposes of the Library of Congress.[7] A single deposit can satisfy both of these requirements, but in order for it to do so, it must be made at the same time that the registration application is filed or be accompanied by a letter asking the Copyright Office to hold it until the registration application is filed.[8] If deposit is not made under one of these two circumstances, the Copyright Office will forward it to the Library of Congress, and you will have to make a separate deposit when you register your copyright.

Deposit with the Library of Congress can be required even if you have no desire or intention to register your copyright. If the Librarian of Congress decides that the Library should have a copy or copies of your work, the Register of Copyrights will send you a written demand for deposit. You have three months to comply; if you do not, you will be liable for a fine of $250 and for any expenses incurred by the Library of Congress in acquiring copies of your work. If your failure to comply is willful or repeated, you may also be liable for an additional fine of $2,500.[9]

The following rules govern deposit with the Library of Congress:[10]

1. Only published works will be held by the Library. Unpublished works may have to be deposited for registration purposes, but not for purposes of the Library of Congress unless by some special arrangement between the author and the Library.

2. The following types of published works are exempt from deposit with the Library:

• Scientific or technical diagrams and models. Architectural plans, blueprints, and models are covered by this exemption.

• Greeting cards, picture postcards, and stationery.

• Lectures, sermons, speeches, and addresses unless they are published in an anthology or collection. Anthologies and collections are not exempt from deposit, even if all the contents are the work of one person.

• Literary, dramatic, or musical works on which phonorecords are based, unless those works are also published. In other words, if a sound recording is made of a piece of music, for example, but the music itself is never published in print form, the fact that the sound recording is published in the form of phonorecords does not subject the underlying musical work to the deposit requirement.

• Literary works (such as computer programs) that are published only in such a form that they cannot be perceived by a human being without being translated by a computer or other machine.

• Sculptural works.

• Works embodied only in useful articles or in jewelry, dolls, toys, games, or plaques. For example, if a design is published only by being printed on textiles, it is exempt from deposit for the Library of Congress. Maps and globes are not defined as useful articles and do not come within this exemption.

• Advertising material, including labels.

• Tests and answer material for tests, if published separately from other literary works.

• Works that were first published as contributions to collective works. The collective works themselves are not exempt, only the individual contributions.

• Musical or other works that are published only in movie soundtrack form. This exemption is very similar to that concerning literary, dramatic, or musical works published only in phonorecord form. It means that if a musical work, for example, is not published except in a movie soundtrack, no separate deposit requirement applies to it.

• Television programs whose only publication has been by virtue of a license granted to a nonprofit organization, permitting the organization to make videotapes of it.

3. For published works that are not covered by one of these exemptions, the general rule is that you must deposit two copies of the "best edition." (The current standards for determining what is the "best edition" are reprinted in appendix C.) However, there are certain kinds of works for which a single copy of the best edition will suffice:

• Two-dimensional visual works, so long as no more than four copies of the work have been published, or, if more than four copies have been, the publication has been in the form of a limited edition of no more than three hundred, of which every copy is numbered. If your work qualifies for this special one-copy arrangement, you can also satisfy the deposit requirements by depositing photographs or "other identifying material" instead.

• Motion pictures but not other audiovisual works. Also, with regard to motion pictures, it is possible to enter into a "Motion Picture Agreement" with the Library, permitting you to ask for immediate return of your

deposit copy on the stipulation that the Library may demand it back at any time in the following two years.
• Globes, relief maps, and other three-dimensional cartographic works.
• Musical works published only by rental, lease, or lending but not by sale.
• Multimedia instructional kits. Multimedia for these purposes means anything involving literary works, audiovisual works, and sound recordings, or any combination of two of these types.

4. Works published in the form of holograms are covered by special rules. In addition to two copies, you must deposit two sets of precise instructions for displaying the image and two sets of photographs or other material that will identify the image.

5. If you are depositing copies of a phonorecord, you must deposit with it any label or package on or in which it is usually sold.

6. The Register of Copyrights, in conjunction with the Library of Congress, can grant special absolution from the deposit requirement if you can give persuasive reasons why your work should be exempted. If you wish for such treatment, you must submit your request (and your reasons) in writing to the Chief of the Acquisitions and Processing Division of the Copyright Office. Any request must be signed by either the owner of the underlying copyright or the owner of the publication right. Thus the owner of a derivative work right cannot apply on his own to have the work exempted from any deposit requirements.

7. If you would like a receipt for your deposit, you can obtain one by paying a $2 fee.

The rules governing deposit for registration purposes are slightly different. For one thing, there are no exemptions; deposit is an absolute prerequisite for registration. There are differences in the deposit requirements between one type of work and another, and some of these differences are similar to those in the Library of Congress context, but you should be very careful not to confuse deposit for registration with deposit for the Library.

The rules for registration deposit are as follows.[11]

1. Only one copy is required to register an unpublished work. (A motion picture is not considered to be published merely because a nonprofit institution has been given a license to make a fixation of it. For example, if a school is given permission to videotape a television broadcast, the television program is still unpublished for deposit purposes though not for other purposes.)

2. As with Library of Congress deposit, the basic rule for published works is that you must submit two copies of the best edition. However, one copy of the best edition will suffice for these types of published works:

• Two-dimensional visual works, so long as no more than four copies have been published, or, if more than four have been published, so long as publication has been in the form of an edition limited to 300 or fewer, all copies being numbered. Any visual work qualifying for this one-copy arrangement can also be deposited in the form of photographs or other identifying material.

• Motion pictures but not other audiovisual works.

• Globes, relief maps, and other three-dimensional cartographic works.

• Scientific or technical diagrams. Architectural plans and blueprints come under this exception.

• Greeting cards, picture postcards, and stationery.

• Lectures, sermons, and similar material published individually and not as part of a collective work.

• Contributions to a collective work. The deposit for registration of a contribution to a collective work should be of a copy of the collective work as a whole.

• Music published only in sheet form, or if in phono-records, only by rental, leasing, or lending.

• Multimedia instructional lists.

• Advertising materials, including labels. If one of these was published in a magazine or other periodical, it is sufficient to deposit just the page of the periodical on which it appeared, not the entire pediodical. If a print or label is physically inseparable from a three-dimensional object—for example, if it is stamped on the base of the object—different rules apply. (See point 4 below.)

• Tests and answer material for tests, if published separately from other literary works.

• Designs that are published only by being printed on textiles, wallpaper, wrapping paper, and similar merchandise. If the design is repeated on the material, the swatch submitted for deposit must show at least one repetition. However, if the only way that the design is published is by the incorporation of the textiles (or what-have-you) in dresses, furniture, or other three-dimensional articles, different rules apply.

• Works first published abroad. In such a case, the one copy deposited should be a copy of that first foreign edition, not a copy of the best edition.

3. You can make deposit in the form of identifying material rather than in the form of a copy or copies for certain kinds of works:

• Unpublished two-dimensional visual works.

• Published two-dimensional visual works, so long as no more than four copies have been published, or, if more than four have been, so long as publication has been in the form of an edition limited to 300 or fewer, all copies being numbered.

• Unpublished motion pictures (but not other kinds of audiovisual works).

• Unpublished works fixed only in motion picture soundtracks.

• Works that are published only in the form of motion picure soundtracks.

4. For certain kinds of works, the only proper deposit for registration purposes is in the form of "identifying material":

• Sculptural works, models, and maquettes.

• Computer programs and data bases (see appendix D).

• Unpublished visual works that are fixed only in useful articles, or in jewelry, toys, dolls, or games.

• Published visual works, if they are published only in useful articles or in jewelry, toys, dolls, or games. This category includes visual works that are published only by virtue of the fact that the textile or other material on which they are printed is used in making a three-dimensional article. For example, if a design is printed on fabric used to upholster chairs, and the only manner by which the design is published is the sale of chairs upholstered in that material, then deposit must be made in the form of identifying material. Neither this category nor the previous one includes visual works that are embodied in useful articles that are part of a multimedia educational or instructional kit.

• Works for which the copy deposited would be larger than eight feet in length, width, or height.

• Advertising material that is physically inseparable from a three-dimensional article. For example, if the design of a label is stamped into the base of a lamp, to copyright the label design you must make deposit in the form of identifying material.

5. There is a special additional requirement for motion pictures, whether published or unpublished. If you deposit in the form of a copy or copies, you must also submit a synopsis or some other description of the contents of the motion picture.

6. There are also special benefits given to motion pictures. First, the Library of Congress is given thirty days from the effective date of registration (the date on which registration, deposit, and fee are received) to decide whether it wishes to keep the copy or copies that have been deposited for registration. If it does not make a decision within thirty days or if it decides it does not want the motion picture for its archives, the copy or copies will be returned to the applicant. Second, as an alternative to this you can enter into a Motion Picture Agreement such as I have described above. Third, the Copyright Office will accept motion picture soundtracks as deposits for purposes of registering simultaneously all works contained in them, including music.

7. There is a special additional requirement for holograms. For each copy submitted, you must also submit precise instructions for displaying the image and some kind of material clearly showing the image.

8. The Register of Copyrights can permit you to deposit one copy instead of two, or to deposit an incomplete copy or copies, if you can present a convincing reason why you should receive special treatment. A request for special treatment must be signed by the applicant. (This signature rule is less strict than that for the Library of Congress deposit.) To make such a request, write to the Chief of the Examining Division of the Copyright Office. This is a different person from the person to whom you submit such requests in the Library of Congress context. You can combine the two requests; if you do so, the Chief of the Examining Division is the person to address, and the application must be signed either by the owner of the underlying copyright or by the owner of the publication right.

The identifying material which can be used to satisfy the deposit requirement is a photograph, transparency, drawing, photocopy, or any other two-dimensional reproduction or rendering of the work. For example, a photograph of a limited-edition woodcut or a drawing of a sculptural work will suffice. There are a few special rules:[12]

• Material reproducing two-dimensional visual works must reproduce the actual colors of the work. This is not true of material reproducing sculptural works.

• If you submit more than two pieces of material for any one work, all must be the same size.

• Transparencies must be 35mm and must be mounted in cardboard, plastic, or similar materials. All other types of material must be not less than five by seven inches and not more than nine by twelve inches, the preferred size is eight by ten inches.

• Except in the case of transparencies, the image must be at least life-size, except that it can be less than life-size if it is at least four inches in any one dimension.

• At least one piece of identifying material must indicate the title of the work and the exact measurement of at least one of the true dimensions of the work.

• If the work is published, at least one piece of material must show the copyright notice. If the notice is so placed on the work that a photograph or other reproduction will not show it, you must submit a separate drawing showing the exact appearance, location, size, and content of the notice.

• These rules do not apply to unpublished motion pictures or to works that are fixed or published only in the form of a motion picture soundtrack. For unpublished motion pictures, identifying material is composed of a description of the movie, together with either a phonorecord of some kind, reproducing the entire soundtrack, or a set of visual reproductions of single frames—at least one frame from each ten minutes of footage. The description may be a synopsis, a continuity, or anything of that sort, but it must include: the title, and the episode title also, if it is an episode; the nature and general content; the date of first fixation; the date of first transmission; if the work was fixed simultaneously with transmission, a statement to that effect; the running time; and the credits appearing on the work.

Multiple Registration

Because of the $10 filing fee, it would in many cases be a burden to the author to have to register separately every work he has created. Fortunately an exemption from the rigors of registration has been given to individual authors (but not joint authors) who contribute to periodicals.[13] An individual author may now register on a single form (form GR/CP), and for a single fee, all works published in periodicals (including newspapers) in a given 12-month period, provided that:

1. Each of the works, on the occasion of its first publication, bore a separate copyright notice (separate, that is, from the general copyright notice on the periodical), and each notice identified the author in the same manner (for example, not by name in one issue and by pseudonym in another).

2. You attach one copy of each periodical (or, in the case of a newspaper, one copy of the relevant section of each newspaper) to your application.

3. You identify each work on your application form and state the name and date of the periodical issue in which it first appeared. (Slightly different rules apply if the registration is for renewal of copyright in contributions to periodicals published before January 1, 1978.)

Group registration such as this requires filing two forms: form VA, PA, or TX, depending on the type of work that your contributions happen to be, and form GR/CP. The VA, PA, or TX will contain all information except the titles of the works and the statistics of their publication; these facts will be put on the GR/CP.

Can You Register More Than Once?

It is possible under certain circumstances that you may wish to make a second registration of a work. In fact, in the case of a work that you first registered when it was still unpublished, you will be well advised to register again when you publish it if you have changed the title. You will also want to make a second registration if the first registration was not made in the name of the true copyright claimant, or if the original registration was for some other reason unauthorized or legally invalid—for example, if it was made by someone not entitled to make it. However, these are the only circumstances in which the same version of a work may be registered more than once.

Correcting an Erroneous or Incomplete Registration

After you have registered, you may wish to correct certain information contained in your registration or to supply additional information. This may be done by filing form CA, the application for supplementary registration, along with a $10 fee. No additional deposit need be made. Supplementary registration does not change the legal validity of the original registration. Because of this, supplementary registration may not be used for adding to a list of works covered by a previously filed group registration. It may not be used to record transfers of copyright ownership. Nor is it an appropriate way to notify the Copyright Office of changes in the content of your work. If the content has changed so much as to constitute a new version, you should make a new registration, and if it has not, your old registration remains valid. Nor is it the right procedure to use if the original registration was made in the name of someone who was not the proper copyright claimant; in such a case, a new registration must be made. Minor errors in the name of the copyright claimant, however, can and should be corrected by supplementary registration. Also, form CA is sometimes used as a way of getting on the Copyright Office's index the titles of stories, songs, or other works that have been registered already but as parts of a collective work.

An application for supplementary registration may be made by the author, by anyone who has become a copyright claimant by dint of having received the underlying claim from the author, by the owner of any subsidiary right in the work, or by an authorized agent of any of these.

Reproduction of Works for the Blind and Handicapped

Space 8 on form TX (for nondramatic literary works) deals with reproduction of your work "for the use of blind or physically handicapped persons." Completing this part of the form is purely voluntary. By completing it you give the Library of Congress a special nonexclusive license to reproduce your work for the benefit of the blind and the handicapped. This reproduction may be in braille, in phonorecords that are specially designed for use by the blind and the handicapped, or in both media; the choice is up to you.

The terms of this nonexclusive license are as follows:[14]

1. It can be granted only for works that have already been published.

2. It can be granted only by a person who owns the exclusive publication right or the exclusive right to make a sound recording of a work.

3. The Library of Congress assumes the burden of ensuring that every copy or phonorecord carries proper copyright notice.

4. The license, being nonexclusive, does not prevent you, as the owner of the publication or sound recording right, from making other nonexclusive licenses of your

right. You can even make an exclusive license, or an absolute sale, of your right, subsequent to this, but whoever takes that exclusive license takes it subject to the special Library of Congress license.

5. The license will last for the duration of the copyright, unless it is terminated before that.

6. Termination can be made at any time, unlike termination of other nonexclusive licenses. You must give the Library of Congress at least ninety days' notice. In order to terminate, send a signed statement to the Library of Congress's Division for the Blind and Physically Handicapped. Once termination goes into effect, the Library cannot make any more copies or phonorecords, but it can continue to use the ones it has already made.

7. Someone who purchases an exclusive publication or sound recording right subject to this license can terminate the license in the same way.

8. After termination, the license can be given again, by filing a form CA for supplementary registration.

Certificate of Registration   When the Register of Copyrights approves your application for registration, or for supplementary registration, the Copyright Office will issue you a certificate of registration, or a certificate of supplementary registration. The certificate has no separate legal significance, but it is useful to have it in your possession in case the official record of your registration is misplaced by the Copyright Office. Moreover, in subsequent transfers and other contracts involving the copyright, it will prove convenient to refer to the certificate since it contains, or should contain, the exact description of the copyright. It will also inform you of the registration number, to which you will want to refer when making or terminating transfers of copyright. (The registration number will be changed if a supplementary registration is made.) Additional copies of the certificate can be obtained from the Copyright Office for $4 each.

6

Rights in Copyrighted Works

One of the many respects in which copyright resembles property in land is that of divisibility. If you own a parcel of land, you can sell mineral rights to *A*, water rights to *B*, and a right of way to *C*, and still be considered the owner of the underlying property. Copyright too can be exploited in many different ways. It comprises five basic rights, which, along with certain limitations and exceptions, are set forth in the statute.

The Right to Copy

The right to copy is the right to reproduce the work in copies or phonorecords. With regard to sound recordings, this right is limited. Someone else is free to make a recording that blatantly imitates yours; only if he actually lifts sounds from your recording is he infringing. This rule shows practical wisdom. Two renditions of a symphony are bound to sound alike; it would stifle artistic competition to require performers to differentiate themselves in unproductive ways.

The statute also limits to some degree the exclusivity of the right to copy computer programs. It provides that anyone who is an "owner" of a copy of a computer program may make an object code copy of it, so as to be able to use it in a computer. Such a copy may not, however, be transferred unless the original copy is also transferred, and unless the owner is also transferring whatever rights he may have in the program. The owner is also permitted to make copies for archival purposes, so long as the archival copies are destroyed when continued possession of the program "should cease to be rightful."[1]

Curiously, the statute does not in so many words require destruction of the object code version when possession of the program ceases to be rightful, but one can only presume that this was an oversight, and that any cessation of rights in the program would cover all copies made, as well as copies originally received.

It is not clear why these provisions were added to the statute at all. It is hard to believe that the concept of fair use, which I will discuss in chapter 8, would not permit anyone in rightful possession of a program to take whatever steps might be necessary to make full use of it. Even more obscure, and more troubling, is the limitation of these statutory rights to the "owner" of a copy of a program, and the apparent exclusion of a lessee. Did Congress intend to say, by negative implication, that inputting a program would not be permissible for a lessee without specific authorization? One certainly hopes not, but the legislative history is ambiguous. As originally proposed by CONTU, this provision of the statute spoke of "possessors," not owners. Somehow, somewhere, the word was changed, and there is no public record as to why.

As I have mentioned, the law regards an object code version of a computer program as a copy of the program, not a derivative work. There seems no reason not to apply this to data bases as well. For example, inputting an English-language directory into a computer data base would be copying it, not "translating" it into a new language. In fact, the same rationale would apply to the making of a computer-readable version of any work. Thus, no one who makes a computer-readable version of any public domain work would have any copyright in it, unless some new elements are added. On the other hand, translating a computer program from one computer language to another would probably create a derivative work—assuming of course that anything survived the process other than the ideas or algorithms of the original.

The Right to Create Derivative Works

The general concept of "derivative works" has already been discussed. As with the right to copy, this right has also been limited by statute where computer programs are concerned. The "owner" of a copy of a program is entitled to adapt it to his own needs, but may not transfer the adaptation except with the consent of the copyright owner in the original. Again, it seems unnecessary to have provided this in the statute, since the concept of fair use is surely broad enough to protect this kind of activity. Also, the limitation of the statute to "owners" ought not to be read as depriving lessees of a similar right.

As for sound recordings, the only derivative work that is covered by copyright is a rearrangement of the actual sounds of the recording.

It is possible to make a derivative work of a derivative work, but, as I have mentioned above, anyone doing this should take great care to obtain all necessary permissions. If, for example, a company wishes to make dolls based on a movie character, it must buy the right to do so not only from the person who owns the movie rights but also, if the character in the movie was based on a novel or a cartoon, from the novelist or cartoonist as well.

The Right to Distribute Copies or Phonorecords to the Public

This is the right to publish, and needs no elaboration.

The Right to Perform the Work Publicly

"Publicly" in this case means outside the normal circle of family and social acquaintances. "Perform" includes both live performance and indirect performance by means of electronic broadcasting and similar processes. In the case of a movie or other audiovisual work, to perform the work means to show it by means of a projector or any other device.

The right to perform a work includes the right to have phonorecords of that work played in public. The owner of a copyright in the sound recording does not possess this right of performance; it belongs to the author of the underlying work.[2] For example, if you have written a song and a singer has made a record of it, you are the person who controls the playing of the record in public; the singer has no voice in the matter. Of course you can sell the performance right to the singer if you wish, but the two rights are separate.

What, then, of a videotape, which in theory seems indistinguishable from a sound recording? Alas, there is no logical consistency here. If you permit someone to make a videotape of a play you have written, that person, not you, controls public performance of the videotape. There is no logical reason for applying this principle to audiovisual derivative works and not to sound recordings. The causes of the inconsistency are more powerful than logic though; they have their roots in history. Consequently the rule is like certain rules of grammar that you can only memorize and should not struggle to understand.

The law permits certain types of performances in spite of copyright. These exceptions are elaborately defined.[3]

An exception is created for performances by nonprofit educational institutions in the course of face-to-face teaching activities. A performance in a Berlitz classroom, for example, would infringe the copyright because Berlitz schools are commercial, not nonprofit. This exception does not apply to performance of audiovisual works if the person performing the work knows, or has reason to know, that the copy being used is an unlawful copy. Thus, for example, a teacher cannot show a film that she suspects was pirated.

An exception is also created by law for the use of radios or television sets in public places, provided that the equipment is the standard type normally found in private homes and that no separate charge is made to the audience. A common example is the television in your neighborhood saloon; if the customers are not charged for the privilege of watching and if the television is an ordinary kind (not one with a five-by-five-foot screen) the bartender is not regarded as "performing" any of the broadcast works.

A related exception covers the cable systems used by hotels and apartment houses, which connect all of the rooms or apartments to a common antenna. Cable systems used by governmental bodies or nonprofit institutions are also exempted, so long as they are not used for any sort of commercial advantage, charge no more than enough to meet expenses, and are available either to anyone who wants to hook into the system or only to private viewers or listeners.[4]

Other exceptions are created by law for performances of nondramatic literary or musical works. The first is for educational broadcasts. It covers broadcasts whether on the air or by cable, so long as they are a regular part of the educational program of a nonprofit educational institution or a governmental body. A broadcast must be made primarily for reception in classrooms or "similar places normally devoted to instruction" (which, for handicapped persons, may mean their own homes) or on governmental premises. Interestingly, the school or governmental body making any such broadcast is free to make up to thirty copies of the program, so long as all but one archival copy are destroyed within seven years.[5] Just what can be done with the copies is unclear, but it seems fair to say that any educational use within the institution or agency would be all right.

A performance of such a work not for commercial profit is also outside the scope of copyright. However, for a performance to fit under this exception, there must be no admission charge—or the profits must go to charity—and no compensation may be paid to any performer, producer, or promoter. Both of these conditions must be met: a free concert will be a copyright infringement if the performer receives any payment beyond reimbursement of expenses.

The privilege given to charitable benefit performances has one other important qualification. It is still possible for the owner of the basic copyright, or the owner of the exclusive performance right in a work, to prevent such a performance, if he gives written notice of objection to the promoters or other persons responsible at least a week in advance.[6] The notice must comply with two rules.

First, it must be signed by the copyright owner or by the performance right owner, or by someone empowered to act on behalf of one of them, and the signature must be dated and accompanied by the name, address, and telephone number of the signer, printed legibly or typed. The notice must include this information:

1. Reference to the statutory authority on which you rely. The statute should be cited. It is 17 U.S.C. §110(4).

2. The date and place of the performance that you object to, or, if you do not know this information exactly, then as much information as you do know about it, as well as your source, unless your source is confidential.

3. The reasons for your objection.

4. Clear identification, by title and at least one author, of the work you do not want performed, or, if you prefer, a blanket identification of a group of works that have something in common, which can be as general as being written by the same author or published by the same publisher. If you choose the blanket-notice route, you must give the name, address, and telephone number of at least two persons from whom the other party can obtain a more specific identification of the works. Also, if your notice does not identify the copyright or performance-right owner or owners of all the works, you must offer to provide that information, including names and last known addresses.

5. A statement that the persons will be free to go ahead with the performance if no admission charge is made and if no profit inures to the performers or the promoters, but that otherwise those persons may be liable for copyright infringement.

Second, the notice must be received at least a week before the performance. You can instead give brief notice by telegram, if you get a signed letter with all the above information to the proper party before the performance.

Three other exceptions for performances of nondramatic literary or musical works have been made: where the performance takes place as part of a service of religious worship, where the performance is at an agricultural or horticultural fair, and where the performance takes place at a function organized and promoted by a nonprofit veterans' organization or fraternal organization. In the second case, you may in fact sue the performers, but not the governmental or other nonprofit body that sponsors the fair. The third exception only applies if the general public is not invited to the performance and if the organization uses any proceeds (after paying reasonable production costs) exclusively for charitable purposes. It is designed, in short, to permit the local VFW or Elks or what have you to hold a fundraiser for their members without paying royalties. It does not, by the way, extend to college fraternities or sororities unless the performance is held to raise money for charitable purposes that are specified in advance.

In addition, the law has carved out some rather specialized exceptions. A dramatic musical work (such as opera or a ballet) may be performed in a religious service. A nondramatic musical work may be performed in a store for purposes of advertising sheet music or phonorecords. And a nondramatic literary work may be broadcast to blind, deaf, or other handicapped persons by a governmental body, a public broadcasting station, a cable system, or a radio subcarrier. Either of the first two can make up to ten copies of the program and keep them on hand for this purpose or lend them to similar organizations for the same purpose.[7]

The only exception created for performances of dramatic literary works, such as plays, is in the case of performances for the benefit of people who cannot read normally. Such a performance may not be made for profit, may be made only once by any one group of performers or under the aegis of any one organization, and may only be made of works that were first published at least ten years previously.

The Right to Display the Work Publicly

Display, like performance, includes broadcasting and other mechanical forms of communication. Where audiovisual works are concerned, display should not be confused with performance: you perform a film by playing it in the usual way; you display a film by projecting isolated frames.

The display right is a significant change from prior law and is of great importance to artists working in the visual arts. Someone who buys a painting has the right to place the work on exhibit in a museum or to display it to the public in any other way, so long as the public are physically present at the place of display. But the buyer has no right, unless he specifically buys the right from the artist, to broadcast an image of the painting or permit anyone else to broadcast it. Moreover this limited right to display a painting is given only to buyers; people who rent, borrow or lease works of art have no right to display them in any way outside the circle of their friends and guests.

Like the performance right, the right to control display of a work does not extend to display in nonprofit or governmental educational situations. (However, as with performance, this does not give a teacher the right to display a copy of an audiovisual work if he knows or has reason to believe that the copy was unlawfully made.) Nor does the right to control display extend to display by a hotel proprietor or someone of that sort if all he uses to display the work is an ordinary television set and if he charges nothing to the public for the privilege of seeing the display.[8]

Exceptions are also made for display in a service of religious worship[9] and display, in an advertisement or a news report, of a useful work—for example, a pillowcase or a placemat—that lawfully incorporates a work of visual art.[10] Thus, if a painter licenses a wildlife painting to a maker of plastic placemats, the maker can advertise the placemats without infringing the painter's display right.

Other Rights in Visual Works

In many European countries, and especially in France, the law has long protected artists even beyond the sale of their works, by what is known as the *droit de suite* and *droit moral*. *Droit de suite* is the right to share in the profits of future sales of a work; when a work is sold by one collector to another, the artist gets a portion of the profit made by the seller. *Droit moral* (loosely translated as "moral right") is the right to control alterations of the work, and the right to be acknowledged as its author if one chooses.

Federal law in this country does not include anything comparable, and artists have fared poorly trying to persuade courts that such rights should exist. However, two states—New York and California—have now enacted moral right statutes for works of fine art other than those commissioned for commercial purposes.[11] New York prohibits the display or publication of a work with attribution to the artist, if the work has been "altered, defaced, mutilated, or modified" without the artist's approval. The artist is also given a right to be recognized as the author of his or her works, or even, for good cause, to disclaim authorship and have any attribution removed. California's statute goes further; it gives the artist a cause of action against the owner of a work who alters or defaces it and also prohibits destruction of the work without the artist's consent.

California alone has also enacted a *droit de suite* statute, giving artists certain percentages on resales of their works.[12] It remains to be seen whether this statute will, as some curmudgeons have predicted, merely drive the California art market into neighboring states.

In time the moral right, if not the *droit de suite*, will probably become more widely accepted in this country. It can coexist peacefully with the copyright law; however, artists should be aware of one pitfall. If an artist has granted away all copyright interests in a work, the grantee will be entitled under federal law to make derivative works based on it. This right would, presumably, override any state law preventing alteration; alternatively, the two could be reconciled by treating the grant as a blanket "consent" to the alteration. In either case, the artist will probably be out of luck.

7

Implicit in the ownership of property is the privilege of determining who reaps the profits of it and what those profits will be. This is true of copyright no less than of other kinds of property. But in recent decades our laws have tended to make exceptions to this privilege; in the case of copyright, these are the so-called compulsory licenses.

The Phonorecord License

The first of the four compulsory licenses affects the right to make and distribute phonorecords of nondramatic musical compositions. In essence, once phonorecords of a piece of music have been distributed to the public in the United States (and remember that a movie soundtrack is not a phonorecord), any other person may make another sound recording of the work and distribute phonorecords of his recording.[1] Moreover, and more importantly, the artist who records the work under a compulsory license may arrange the music, though not the accompanying words, so as to suit his own style or interpretation, if he does not change the basic melody or what the statute calls, with admirable complacency, the "fundamental character" of the work. What "fundamental character" means, no one knows. Most probably this will be decided on a case-by-case basis. Certainly this section of the statute is likely to furnish the grounds of litigation.

To obtain a compulsory license, one must serve notice by registered or certified mail on whoever owns the underlying copyright in the musical work. If there are two or more owners, only one needs to be served.[2] If the records of the Copyright Office do not identify the copyright owner or do not give an address, or if the last known address yields no results, notice may be served instead on the Copyright Office. If the person seeking the compulsory license does not serve notice one way or another before distributing any phonorecords or within thirty days after he makes his first phonorecord, he cannot obtain a compulsory license, and his phonorecords will be copyright infringements.

At the top, the notice should bear the legend, "Notice of Intention to Obtain a Compulsory License for Making and Distributing Phonorecords." It should state the title of the work and the names of the author or authors, so far as they are known. It should contain the following information about the person or entity seeking the license:[3]

1. The full legal name. All trade names and stage names used in the record business should also be listed, even if they are not going to be used in connection with this particular work. For example, if Bridget Mahoney, known to the world as Wanda Waverly, intends to take out the license, she should list both her names.

2. The full and complete business address used in the record business. A post office box number or similar address is not sufficient unless there is no street address.

3. A statement of the type of business organization used in connection with the record business—for example, individual proprietorship, partnership, corporation, or charitable foundation. Publicly traded companies must identify themselves as such; other cor-

porations must list their directors and officers and the names of every stockholder owning 25 percent or more of their stock. (The true beneficial owner is what is wanted here; if the stock is held by a trustee for someone else's benefit, the beneficiary's name must be given.) Every noncorporate organization must list the names of every true owner (beneficial owner) of 25 percent or more of the enterprise, and if any of these is an organization, it has to be identified in the same way as for actual licensees. Suppose that a private individual forms a joint venture with a corporation to make records. The joint venture is the licensee, but the corporation's officers, directors, and so forth must still be listed.

4. The accounting year. For example, if a company seeking the license keeps its books and pays its taxes on a June 30 fiscal year, that must be stated.

5. Every type of phonorecord that the licensee will publish, including cassette, cartridge, or reel-to-reel.

6. The intended date of publication.

7. The name of the principal recording artist or group that is or will be involved.

8. The catalog number or numbers that published phonorecords will bear.

The notice has to be signed, and the name of the person signing has to be legibly printed.

If you are the copyright owner in the musical work, you will not receive any royalties under the compulsory license until the copyright has been registered and any other documents necessary to identify you have been recorded. However, these filings are not onerous, and they are all you need to do to receive a compulsory license royalty.

The amount of the royalty to be paid on each phonorecord distributed under a compulsory license between January 1, 1983 and June 30, 1984 is either $.0425 for each separate work on the phonorecord or $.008 per minute of playing time for each separate work, whichever is larger. From July 1, 1984 through December 31, 1985, these rates go up to $.045 and $.085, respectively, and thereafter to $.05 and $.095, respectively. Royalties must be paid every month, on or before the twentieth day of the month. Once a year, every person making phonorecords under a compulsory license must send to the copyright owner an accounting statement showing his calculations of how many phonorecords he has distributed and any other relevant information. Failure to pay royalties on a monthly basis and to file accounts when they are due can result in loss of the license.

It is important to remember that royalties are to be paid to the copyright owner. This is the person who owns the sound recording right in the musical work, for that is the right that is being sublicensed to others. In almost all cases this will be the composer or someone who has obtained the basic copyright from the composer.

There are several qualifications to the compulsory license:

1. It may be obtained only if the primary purpose of producing phonorecords under it is to distribute them to the public for private use. Phonorecords made primarily for broadcasting or for background music systems cannot be made under a compulsory license. They must be expressly authorized by the copyright owner. However, sale of a phonorecord to a broadcaster, if the phonorecord is available to the general public, would not invalidate the compulsory license.

2. It may be obtained only if the original phonorecords were distributed with the permission of the owner of the underlying copyright in the music. In other words, if a phonorecord of a musical composition is

made without the consent of the copyright owner, the distribution of such a phonorecord, being an infringement, does not give rise to a compulsory license in anyone else.

3. The compulsory license does not permit a subsequent producer simply to duplicate a recording made by someone else.

4. Every sound recording made under a compulsory license is copyrightable as a derivative work. But an arrangement of the music, made to suit the style or interpretation of a particular performer, does not qualify as a derivative work and cannot be copyrighted.

5. The compulsory license may be lost if royalties are not paid on time and if the required monthly and yearly statements of account are not sent to the copyright owner on time. In the case of such a default, the copyright owner may give written notice to the licensee, and if the matter is not remedied within thirty days, the license will terminate. If the license terminates, continuing to make or distribute phonorecords will be regarded as infringement of the copyright.

I should add that many performers do not go through the complexities of obtaining a compulsory license but instead deal directly with the copyright owner or with the Harry Fox Agency, Inc., a large phonorecord license clearinghouse located in New York City. "Harry Fox licenses," as they are called, are sometimes cheaper than the statutory license.

The Jukebox License

Until the new law went into effect on January 1, 1978, the performance of a nondramatic musical work by means of a jukebox was not considered an infringement of the performing right in the work unless the place where the jukebox was located charged an admission fee. The new law has ended this unconscionable state of affairs.[4]

Because jukeboxes are so widespread and owned by so many hundreds of companies, it would be inefficient for jukebox owners and composers to negotiate directly with each other. Instead the law requires jukebox owners to pay a fee each year for each jukebox. This fee is currently $50 ($25 for a half year) with a cost-of-living adjustment likely to be applied in 1987 and thereafter. Fees are paid to the Copyright Office, which in turn transfers the funds to the U.S. Treasury. Distribution of the money to composers is carried out by the Copyright Royalty Tribunal.

The Copyright Royalty Tribunal is a new institution established by Congress as part of the legislative branch. It has an advisory role and also certain less enviable tasks, such as this one of dividing up compulsory license royalties. The Tribunal is composed of five members, serving staggered seven-year terms. The members are appointed by the President of the United States, subject to the approval of the Senate. Among its other powers, it has authority to hold hearings to sort out conflicting claims to the kitty of license royalties. Any determination it makes on these claims can be appealed to a U.S. Court of Appeals.

If you are the composer of a musical work and have reason to feel that your work is currently being performed on jukeboxes, all you need to do to obtain a share of the license fees is to file a claim with the Copyright Royalty Tribunal in January of the following year. If you are a member of ASCAP, Broadcast Music, Inc., SESAC, Inc., or any other performing rights society, you should not make the claim yourself but through the society. Once a year after October 1 the Copyright Royalty Tribunal will divide up the revenue from the license fees among the applicants. First it must decide what portion goes to each individual applicant;

what is left is divided among the performing rights societies.

The process of allocating royalties to individual applicants is rather troublesome. If you are an individual applicant, you should attempt to inform the Copyright Royalty Tribunal of your reasons for thinking you are entitled to such-and-such a share of the pot. To do this with thoroughness would consume much time, energy, and money; the most you will be reasonably expected to do is to show that in your local area your work is available in a certain number of jukeboxes. This requires your having access to the jukeboxes. If any jukebox owner tries to forbid you access or denies a reasonable request for information, you may sue in the District of Columbia District Court to have his license revoked and to have his operation of the machine declared an infringement of your copyright. If the proprietor of an establishment where a jukebox is located tries to forbid you access or, after receiving your request by registered or certified mail, refuses to divulge the ownership of his machine, he is potentially liable as a co-infringer of your copyright. These procedures may be costly and time-consuming; they underline the desirability of joining performing rights societies.

Only in two cases can you go directly into federal court and sue for infringement without going through the preliminaries described. The first is if the jukebox does not carry its certificate of license in plain view. The certificate must be placed on the machine, in a visible spot, by March 1 of any given year, unless the box did not begin operation until after the first of the year. In that case the certificate has to be in place, at the latest, two months after operation begins.[5]

The second case in which you can bring suit immediately is the case of a jukebox located in any establishment that charges an admission fee, either directly or indirectly. Jukeboxes in such establishments are not entitled to compulsory licenses, and their performances are infringements.

The Cable Broadcasting License

The third of the compulsory licenses involves performance or display of works by cable television and cable radio. The creation of this compulsory license does not take away from copyright owners anything they had before. On the contrary, it is a long-awaited recognition of their rights. The Supreme Court had held in 1968 that cable transmissions were not "performances" and therefore not infringements of copyright;[6] the new law rectifies this anomaly and provides a new source of revenue for copyright owners in musical works, films, and other broadcast material.

The new statute has clarified the law governing cable television and radio in many ways and has drawn clear lines among cable transmissions that need not obtain a license, those that can acquire a compulsory license, and those that cannot obtain a compulsory license and are by definition infringements (unless specifically authorized).[7]

A cable transmission is an infringement of the performance or display right in a work if any change is made in the program containing the work, or if any change is made in the advertisements that immediately precede or follow the program, or are interspersed in the program. The reason that such alterations constitute infringement is that a cable system that indulges in them is really playing the role of broadcaster, not simply of transmitter, and also is interfering with the justifiable expectations of advertisers. This rule is not absolute; alteration of advertisements is permitted for the purposes of advertising market research, if the research company doing the alteration has obtained the agreement of the advertiser, the broadcaster, and the cable system itself. Also there are certain circumstances under which the Federal Communications Commission permits or even requires alterations of the content of the signals. These exceptions, however, are of minor importance.

Cable transmission will also infringe copyright if it is not "simultaneous," that is, if it is recorded and then transmitted at a later time. The only exception is in the case of cable transmissions made in Alaska, Hawaii, or any U.S. possession or protectorate, and this exception is available only if the videotape copy made by the cable system is performed only once and is not changed in any way, and only if the cable system takes steps to ensure that no duplicate is made of its videotape. (The owner or other officers of the cable system must file a public affidavit that those steps have been taken.)

Cable transmission will also infringe copyright if it is not made available to the general public. Unless required by the FCC, any transmission that is made to a limited group, such as a group of pay-television customers, will infringe copyright unless authorized by the owner of the performance or display right. By this rule, Muzak and similar systems are infringers if they transmit without specific authorization.

Those are the circumstances under which a cable transmission runs the risk of being regarded as an infringer. Unless one of these violations occurs, cable transmission of a network-made program is not regarded as an infringement, and no license of any kind is required for it.

The new compulsory license fee is levied only on the transmission of non-network programs. Although there is no basis in logic for this distinction, it is true that network broadcasting revenues and the royalties that networks pay to copyright owners are structured to reflect the existence of cable transmission, and it is also true that cable extends into very few areas that are not served by one or another affiliate of each major network. Congress decided under these circumstances to leave network broadcasting where it found it. Even within the area of cabling of non-network programs, Congress has made a further limitation: the cable system need pay royalties only for transmissions outside the area served by the broadcaster of the program.

The computation of royalties to be paid by cable systems is extraordinarily complicated. Payment of the royalties, like payment of jukebox royalties, is made to the Copyright Office, but the Copyright Royalty Tribunal is responsible for distribution. If you have reason to believe that a work in which you own the performance or display right is being transmitted by cable system, you must file a claim to that effect with the Copyright Royalty Tribunal during July of any given year. Partly because the computation of royalties is so complicated, the establishment of a claim to part of them will not be easy. If you believe that you are entitled to royalties, you will be well advised to hire a lawyer to present your claim to the Tribunal.

How will you know whether you have a valid claim? Every cable system is required to file a special statement with the Copyright Office twice a year, listing all the broadcasting stations whose broadcasts it has transmitted during the previous six months. This at least will alert you to the possibility that the particular program in which you have an interest has been cabled. Beyond this, you are left more or less to your own devices.

Who is entitled to present the claim? The answer to this question depends on who owns the broadcast performance right in the work or the broadcast display right. If an author has written a play, for example, and sold or licensed to someone an exclusive right to perform that play by means of broadcasting media, the performer is the person who has the right to present a claim, not the author. If, on the other hand, the license is nonexclusive, the author is the person entitled.

In the realm of visual works, the same applies. If you, the artist, have given a television station an exclusive right to display by means of broadcasting, the station has the copyright that counts. On the other hand, if you have given the station only a nonexclusive license, you are the one who should present a claim to the Tribunal.

These rules determine who can present a claim for compulsory license royalties. The rules as to who can sue for infringement are different and more open ended. If an author has sold or licensed his performance or display rights in return for royalties, he can sue the infringer himself, because the infringement affects his income interest. A broadcaster, even one who has only a nonexclusive license, can sue. Furthermore, if the cable system has altered the content of a cabled program, the statute gives every broadcaster in the area where the cable system operates the right to sue, regardless of whether he has any interest whatsoever in the particular copyright being infringed.[8]

In the case of a lawsuit, notice must be given to all persons whose interests in the copyright might be affected. This is, indeed, the general rule for all copyright suits.

The Public Broadcasting License

This license is for the benefit of PBS, National Public Radio, and other noncommercial broadcasters. It is a fairly narrow license, permitting only the performance and display of published nondramatic musical works and the display of published works of art.[9] It also permits a public broadcasting station or network to tape a show where the performance or display occurs and reuse the tape. It is not, however, a license to dramatize a musical work or to make any other kind of derivative work; nor does it extend to display of any compilation of works of art.

The license will supersede any privately negotiated license not recorded with the Copyright Office within thirty days of execution.

Every public broadcaster is required to keep cue sheets and other records concerning its uses under the license, and you as a copyright owner have the right to see them. You are not obliged to take any affirmative steps; the broadcaster will forward your royalties to you. However, if you do not register your copyright, the broadcaster may not know where to find you and after three years will not be obliged to pay you.

The royalty rates are established by the Copyright Royalty Tribunal. The current rates will be in effect until 1988.[10]

8

Infringement and Fair Use

If copyright is like property in land, infringement is like moving onto someone's land without permission, chopping down trees, mining coal, and stealing water from the well. But, unlike boundaries in land, the boundaries of a copyright are never clearly defined and frequently are not known until the end of a lawsuit. I can give, then, only general guidelines for determining those boundaries ahead of time.

Some cases are relatively easy. If an artist claims that someone has performed or displayed his work, or made and sold copies of it without his permission, he has raised a simple question of fact. Either the defendant did these vile deeds, or he did not. The difficult infringement cases are those in which the artist claims that someone else's creation is so like his own that it infringes the underlying copyright in his work.

In the early days of copyright law, the only theft for which the law took retribution was theft of the exact words of a writing. However, as the literary marketplace grew and new forms of literature emerged, and as the public began to pay more attention to the artist and the demands of the artistic ego, this literalism became untenable.[1] In the past few decades it is doubtful if even five infringement suits out of one hundred have charged the defendant with actually using the plaintiff's language, word for word. Suits now are more likely to allege theft of plot, theft of characters, theft of musical theme, and so on. Necessarily in such cases, the courts make judgments that are at least half intuition.

How Does a Court Find Infringement?

The following are some of the factors that a court will consider when someone claims copyright infringement.

Did the defendant see or otherwise have knowledge of the plaintiff's work? If not, he will not be regarded as an infringer. This is the effect of the doctrine of subjective originality, which I have discussed above. Knowledge of a prior work, however, does not have to be conscious: the plaintiff will win if he can prove that the defendant must have been exposed to the work, even though the defendant may honestly have forgotten the event entirely.

Is the plaintiff's work original? This question is closely similar to the previous one, only we are asking now whether the plaintiff himself has a valid copyright on which to sue. If the elements he claims are infringed are things that in fact he took from someone else's work, whether knowingly or not, his copyright claim in those elements is invalid.

Is the plot merely a variation on an old theme, or is it the product of the author's invention? (This question is asked when the suit charges theft of story line.) If it is merely a variation, how closely do the defendant's details track the plaintiff's? Are the details unusual, or are they the sort that anyone would be likely to choose who set out to write a variation on the same old theme? One famous copyright judge has suggested, in the context of the sort of analysis described here, that upon any work "a great number of patterns of increasing generality will fit equally well" and that at some level of generality one should excuse similarity between two works.[2]

Details can be misleading, and to avoid this danger courts will frequently step back some distance and ask, What is the intent of the two works? If characters, for example, or sequences of musical notes, that seem similar in certain particulars are, taken as a whole, quite different from each other, the court will be less likely to find infringement. In considering infringement claims, courts will generally shy away from the type of close textual analysis used in doctoral dissertations; they will look at the two works from the standpoint of an ordinary citizen.[3] This does not mean that they will ignore plagiarism merely because the offending work contains some original matter. A thief is liable for what he has stolen, even if he has possessions of his own; a plagiarist is liable for what he has copied, whether or not he has added to it material of his own invention.[4]

Infringement in the Visual Arts

Where works of visual art are concerned, certain special problems exist. So many piracies that offend our moral sense are not, strictly speaking, infringements. For example, imitation of style, though frequently egregious and irritating, is not infringement unless concrete elements of previous works are plagiarized. The many famous fakes that have been painted in this century, to the extent that they imitate style—brushwork, use of light, type of subject, and so on—and do not actually replicate elements of pictures by the real artist, are not copyright infringements. The fakers may be sued on other grounds—for example, for palming off their works as those of someone else. This is an ordinary action at common law and has nothing to do with copyright.

In the area of visual arts, the problem of subject matter becomes particularly acute. The physical world is, of course, in the public domain. Any number of artists can paint a face, a harbor, or a street without infringing each other's copyrights. As Justice Oliver Wendell Holmes said, "Others are free to copy the original. They are not free to copy the copy."[5] Does this mean that a photographer has no copyright in a simple unfiltered, unretouched photograph of a natural scene? Almost certainly so. Would the answer be different if the angle were unusual? The answer to that is less clear.

Difficulties multiply when we talk of arranged subjects. In a well-known case involving a posed photograph of Oscar Wilde, it was held that a photographer's copyright covers any arrangement he makes of natural objects in order to compose his shot.[6] Should the rule foreclose another photographer from shooting the same subject with different filters and special effects? Or in the realm of painting, should an artist who paints a still life of an identical composition but in a radically different style be considered an infringer? My personal belief is that he should not, but the case has not yet arisen.

Suing the Infringer

An infringer is anyone who violates any of the rights created by law. Suppose you have written a story that someone in Hollywood adapts into a screenplay without your permission. You may sue not only that scriptwriter but also the studio, the film distributors, and the movie theater where the movie is shown.

An infringement suit must be brought in federal court within three years of the time that the infringement took place. Suit on a pre-1978 infringement of common law copyright may still be brought in a state court. This would also apply to any suit based on a work not fixed in a tangible form and so not federally copyrighted.[7] Because the law regards each separate copy, distribution, performance, and so on as a separate infringement, if an infringing book is published in 1980 and you bring suit in 1985, you can receive damages only for copies made or distributed from 1982 on.

You cannot sue for infringement until the work has been registered, and if you are someone other than the author of the work, you cannot sue until you have also recorded the transfer by which you came to own your copyright. If you received your copyright before 1978 by an oral transfer made prior to first publication, you would be exempt from this rule. The statute does not explicitly say so, but this is the only sensible interpretation. Registration, though, would still be required.

Only the person who owns the particular right that has been infringed or who is entitled to royalties from it can sue.[8] Suppose that a playwright has sold stage performance rights in his play to a Broadway producer for $200,000 and has licensed United Artists to make a movie version (a derivative work) in return for a royalty of 2 per cent of profits. Suppose that another film studio has made an unauthorized film based on the play. Who can sue? United Artists can, because it owns the movie rights, and the author can, because he receives royalties from the movie rights. However, the Broadway producer cannot bring suit even though he may stand to lose box office revenues, because he has no ownership interest in the particular right that has been infringed.

For another example, suppose that a singer sets up a trust for the benefit of her child and transfers to it the right to exploit her sound recordings. In such a case, either the trustee or the child can bring suit, because the trustee is the legal owner of the copyright and the child is entitled to the profits.

To return to the example of the play, the fact that the Broadway producer cannot bring suit does not mean that he will never get into court. Quite the contrary.

If his interest is likely to be affected by the outcome of the suit, the law requires that he be given notice of it, and he will then be able, at the court's discretion, to join in the fray. The law requires that notice be given to every person whose interest in the work may be affected, and the court may even require that persons whose claims could not possibly be affected also receive notice. All of these people can join in the lawsuit, if the court permits.[9]

Damages in an infringement suit may take the form of actual damages or of what are called "statutory damages." Actual damages can include lost profits, compensation for injury to reputation, compensation for loss of business opportunity (if you can prove it), and, to the extent they exceed the amount of injury actually done, the profits that the infringer has made.[10]

If at any time during the lawsuit it appears that you will not be able to prove actual damages, you can choose instead to receive statutory damages, which will not be less than $100—and that minimum figure will be applied only if the infringer can prove that he had no reason to believe that he was committing an infringement. If he cannot prove this, damages will be not less than $250 and not more than $10,000, unless you in turn can prove that the infringer committed the infringement willfully; in this case you may be awarded as much as $50,000. (These figures are for all infringements of any one work, by each infringer or group of jointly liable infringers.) The exact amount of statutory damages is in the discretion of the judge or jury.[11]

In addition to damages you may, in the court's discretion, be reimbursed by the infringer for your court costs and also for your attorney's fees. On the other hand, if you lose your lawsuit and the court decides that you had no reasonable grounds for bringing suit in the first place, you may be required to pay the other side's costs and attorneys' fees.[12]

Whether or not you receive damages you may receive injunctive relief, which is to say that the infringer will be prohibited from any further acts of infringement. Such an injunction is good only against the defendant you have brought to court and does not operate against anyone else.

If the infringer infringes willfully and for commercial gain, he can also be prosecuted by the federal government, and if convicted can be fined or sent to jail or both. From these punishments, of course, you will derive only moral compensation. In the event that you yourself are considering undertaking something you know or strongly suspect to be an infringement, be warned that the criminal penalties are severe: up to $25,000 fine in some cases and up to a year in jail.[13] For record or tape piracy the penalties are even greater.

Fair Use

In infringement suits, the two great principles of copyright law almost invariably clash: on one hand, the need to protect the financial interests of creators, to make it worth their while to create; on the other hand, the need to make each person's addition to the sum of human art and knowledge available for the use of all. From this second principle has evolved the concept of "fair use" of copyrighted material. Fair use, as its name makes no attempt to conceal, is not a fixed navigational point; in any given case, much will depend on the judge or jury's instincts.

Underlying the concept of fair use is the problem of economic competition. In English law what we call "fair use" is called "fair dealing"; while that term is inadequate in certain ways, it also captures something important. A use is most likely to be considered permissible if the resulting work does not exploit the commercial value of the original. In this context, the quality or nature of the use becomes of primary concern. Congress has officially recognized this in the new statute. The statute adopts four criteria, developed by courts over many decades, by which a use should be judged fair or unfair:

(1) The purpose and character of the use, including whether such use is of a commercial nature or is for nonprofit educational purposes;

(2) the nature of the copyrighted work;

(3) the amount and substantiality of the portion used in relation to the copyrighted work as a whole; and

(4) the effect of the use upon the potential market for or value of the copyrighted work.[14]

Scholarly quotation is one of the most ancient forms of fair use. The law's interest in propagating knowledge requires that critics, news reporters, and similar persons be allowed to quote from works without paying for the privilege. In an interesting recent case, the writer of a book on "How to Win at Pac-Man" was permitted to use Pac-Man drawings for instructional purposes in the text but not for promotional purposes on the cover.[15] As this case shows, at some point a quotation will cease to be a mere functioning part of the critical text and begin to stand by itself—to be, in short, a copy. As a general rule, a critic or reporter should not quote at any one time more than two or three paragraphs of a book or journal article, a stanza of a poem, a solitary chart or graph from a technical treatise.

Is it fair use for a scholar to quote someone else's work in support of his own thesis rather than for purposes of criticism? To date, no court has had to decide. The custom in the publishing industry is to request permission wherever possible in such cases, and this is certainly the most honorable course. However, it may not always be necessary, so long as credit is given to the author and the quotation is kept to a minimum.[16]

These principles also apply to scholarly use of visual works. Reproduction of an entire painting, even if reduced in size and done in black and white, almost certainly infringes the artist's copyright. However, reproduction of a small portion of a painting for purposes of analyzing the artist's technique would probably constitute a fair use. Displays of works of art in a classroom situation is fair use, as is incidental display or performance in a news broadcast.[17]

Another time-honored fair use, but one less clearly defined, is parody or burlesque. Court after court has wrestled with the question of how much a parodist can appropriate from the original work. To draw too tight a boundary will foreclose the possibility of effective parody, but on the other hand a parody should not be allowed to stray too close to its subject.

One case that in its time caused tremendous controversy is that of *Loew's, Inc.* v. *Columbia Broadcasting System*, in which Jack Benny was sued for his parody of the movie *Gas Light*.[18] The melodramatic mood in *Gas Light* is so splendidly created that it virtually cries out to be parodied. Jack Benny was not one to pass up such an invitation, and his television parody, entitled *Auto Light*, is a grand example of burlesque. The court, however, found Benny's parody to be infringement because the outline of the plot, the characters, the setting, and some dialogue were copied from the original. Well may you ask, how can someone burlesque a work without copying these things? Who would even know the object of the satire, or be instructed by it, were these things omitted?

Posterity has not taken a kindly view of the decision of this case. Nonetheless we must recognize that the judge had to grapple with a difficult problem, for, as he remarked in another case, "The defense, 'I only burlesqued,' . . . is not *per se* a defense."[19] In that other case the judge, trying to set forth the criteria by which a parody must be judged, remarked:

In . . . burlesque a part of the content is used to conjure up, at least the general image, of the original. Some limited taking should be permitted under the doctrine of fair use, in the case of burlesque, to bring about this recalling or conjuring up of the original . . . [The parody] may take an incident of the copyrighted story, a developed character (subject to the limited right of an author in certain situations, . . .) a title (subject to the right of protection [against] unfair competition, . . .) some small part of the development of the story, possibly some small amount of the dialogue.[20]

This list is probably correct and useful so far as it goes, but it omits the important question of the quality, the effect of the use, as distinct from the quantity. For if a copy does not compete with the original—and it would be a strange parody that competed with its subject—then more leeway ought to be allowed in the quantity of the copying. This is certainly the intent of Congress in adopting its four criteria of fair use.

On the other hand, the question of competition may tend to obscure one of the other defenses that a parodist can raise: the right of free speech. Where lies the boundary between copyright and freedom of speech, both of which derive from the Constitution? One's first answer is to say that although a citizen may be free to speak, he is not entitled to speak his mind in the same words as his neighbor. He is free to speak the idea, if you will, but not the expression. However, when you consider that "expression" can mean an arrangement of ideas, this answer wears a bit thin. In the end, discussions on this subject are generally reduced to, "Well, we know what we mean by free speech, even if we can't put it into words."

Not long ago I nearly had to put it into words. A publisher whom I represent had reprinted two speeches by Reverend Sun Myung Moon in a book that was a study of Moon's organization and theology. The book, a collection of scholarly pieces by sociologists and students of religion, showed Moon in rather a bad light. Two satellite organizations of Moon's church—The Bicentennial God Bless America Committee and the International Cultural Foundation— sued the publisher, claiming infringement of copyright.

We had a number of technical defenses—prior publication without notice among them—and as our last line of defense, the First Amendment. I never learned the strength of any of them, though, because both plaintiffs offered to settle out of court.

I have often wondered what would have happened had I raised the issue of the First Amendment. The precedents were not favorable. One that particularly worried me was a case involving a group of Catholic priests who went on tour with their own theologically corrected version of *Jesus Christ Superstar*.[21] Among their defenses to an infringement suit was that the original musical was sick and perverted, and that therefore they were within their First Amendment rights in defending the true faith. The court did not agree. Copying verbatim all but a small fraction of a 2- or 3-hour musical could not be justified in the name of freedom of speech and religion.

On the other hand, there was the case of Abraham Zapruder's movies of President Kennedy's assassination. Zapruder, a Dallas dress manufacturer, had by sheerest chance been aiming his home movie camera at the President's car when the shooting started. He sold his film to *Time* magazine, which later brought suit when someone used various film frames in a book analyzing the assassination. The court in that case held that the use was in the public interest and therefore was a fair use.[22] This was not exactly a First Amendment case, but it came close.

Which precedent would have counted for more in the Moon case I have no idea. I firmly believe that the speeches were of great public importance but, more tellingly, that excerpts or abstracts of them would not have been sufficient. Taken as a whole, the speeches were extraordinary jumbles of disconnected platitudes and logical absurdities, and the essence of what the book's readers deserved to know lay precisely in that.

So, in full knowledge of the risks, I will undertake to put into words a rule for drawing the line between the First Amendment and copyright. My suggestion is this: use of a copyrighted work is fair to the extent that the user could not otherwise convey or demonstrate his ideas in exercise of his freedom of speech.

One area in which copyright has recently had to take a back seat is that of copying for private use. Private use has not been the subject of much litigation; we therefore know little about its legality. We know, for example, that an individual cannot go into a museum and photograph a work of art without permission of the copyright owners, even if he only intends the copy for his personal archives.[23] But what about photographing a work of art that he has bought and rightfully owns? Many of us have assumed that this would be acceptable but without more reason than simply a sense of good sportsmanship. The recent Betamax case has been a welcome confirmation.[24]

The case was brought by Universal Pictures and Walt Disney Productions to prevent Sony from marketing the Betamax machine. The Betamax is a videorecorder that, plugged into a television set, can tape television broadcasts. It is an expensive machine at the moment but, as production technology becomes more effective, will probably be available for far less money in the future. Its future impact on the movie and television industries promises to be tremendous, so Universal and Disney tried to suppress it at the outset.

To do so, they alleged that by selling these machines Sony was a co-infringer of copyright because it provided infringers with tools of piracy. This in itself was a rather farfetched notion. Although it is true that the Betamax is used largely to tape programs off the air, it is also used to play the very videotape cassettes that the plaintiffs were selling. Moreover, although most television programming is under copyright, many old movies are not, and as time goes by more and more material will enter the public domain. Moreover, as the Supreme Court pointed out on appeal, the copyright owners of a majority of television programming do not object to taping, and may even be said to encourage it.

Nevertheless, the District Court chose to make a reply on the merits and to decide whether copying by the purchasers of Betamax machines constituted fair use or infringement. To bring this issue before the court, Universal and Disney had also sued one William Griffiths, a private user of a Betamax machine. Griffiths was a client of the plaintiffs' law firm, was not represented by counsel, and the plaintiffs waived all monetary claims against him. These irregularities the court also chose to overlook, believing the underlying issue to be important and urgent.

The District Court held for the defendants, and on appeal the Supreme Court, overruling the Court of Appeals for the Ninth Circuit by a 5–4 vote, agreed. In part the decision relied upon the fact that the copyright owners of television programs and movies are already compensated by advertising revenues and so are not necessarily harmed. As the District Court noted, Griffiths and other television watchers were not paying a fee for access to the broadcast. Indeed, since advertising revenues are the financial underpinnings of commercial television, "time-shifting" (that is, taping a show so as to be able to watch it at a more convenient time) would seem to benefit, rather than harm, the copyright owner. The Supreme Court found time-shifting to be a fair use and rejected the plaintiffs' argument that they should be able to deny the privilege to their viewers simply because it was, in "amount and substantiality," enormous.

It is hard to say what impact the Betamax case will have on the law in general. The Supreme Court wrote a careful and narrow opinion, emphasizing the peculiar facts of the case. For example, the Court nimbly skirted the issue of "librarying" (that is, retaining copies for an indefinite period), which may more clearly harm copyright owners by cutting into rerun revenues. Thus, the Supreme Court has not given a blanket endorsement to home copying. The one principle we can perhaps extract from the case might be this: for copying, even wholesale copying, in the confines of one's home to be an infringement, harm to the copyright owner must be clear.

Even if this is so, it seems clear that use of the copy must remain personal. No one who has made a copy for his personal use may distribute it to others. Moreover, even if a given individual's use might otherwise be considered personal, this would not necessarily hold true if his copying were part of a community pattern. For example, a company or college might be exposed to risk if it came to light that its members were photocopying works as part of a systematic program for avoiding purchase of the works from the copyright owner.

How does this rule apply to copying done for an individual for a fee? A specific exemption is unofficially given to calligraphers in the congressional report on the new law. (One would not have thought the calligraphers' lobby was so powerful.) If a calligrapher copies a portion of a work, or even the entirety of a very short work such as a poem, for a single individual and does not make a another copy of the same work for any other individual, he will not be considered an infringer.[25]

Congress also makes an exemption, although unofficially, for single copies or phonorecords made without charge for the use of blind persons.[26]

By implication, other copying for private customers is probably not fair use. However, we may never know for certain, because it is not likely to be worth anyone's time and money to sue to prevent it. It is interesting, though, that the agreement recently reached by Gnomon Corporation (a major photocopying company) and the seven publishers that sued it does not mention isolated copying for individuals. The suit between the publishers and Gnomon dealt with a service Gnomon offered under the name of "microprocessing."[27] Gnomon would arrange with university professors to prepare photocopied anthologies of printed works selected by the professors, and sell them to students. This was peculiarly blatant infringement, not at all like sporadic copying for private customers.

What about less directly commercial copying? Businesses and law firms, if they wish to comply with the new law, will have to alter many of their traditional practices. For example, it has been commonplace in the past for a company or firm to take out a single subscription to an expensive newsletter and circulate photocopies through the office. It is highly unlikely that this is still a lawful practice. Indeed most business photocopying, since it is made for commercial advantage, is likely to be an infringement of copyright.[28]

Recently, cases have been brought by publishers against a number of major corporations, including Squibb and American Cyanamid, to stop this and related practices, and have been settled on terms very favorable to the publishers. I would strongly recommend that any business that requires multiple copies of works on a regular basis sign on with the Copyright Clearance Center, of Salem, Massachusetts. The CCC offers an "Annual Authorization Service" for a flat yearly fee, which is computed on the basis of the customer's own self-conducted audit.

The two areas of greatest controversy, the areas where a clear need for public access conflicts with an equally clear need to prevent substantial economic loss to authors, are educational use and library photocopying.

Educational Use, Or, Why Johnny Can't Copy

Photocopying of Literary Works and Works of Art

In working on the new law, Congress attempted to establish a code of conduct for educational photocopying. However, feelings ran so high on the matter that Congress at last shied away. Instead it gave its unofficial approval, in its report on the statute, to a compromise worked out by the Ad Hoc Committee of Educational Institutions and Organizations on Copyright Law Revision, the Authors League of America, Inc., and the Association of American Publishers, Inc. Those guidelines are as follows:[29]

I. *Single Copying for Teachers*

A single copy may be made of any of the following by or for a teacher at his or her individual request for his or her scholarly research or use in teaching or preparation to teach a class:

A. A chapter from a book;
B. An article from a periodical or newspaper;
C. A short story, short essay or short work;
D. A chart, graph, diagram, drawing, cartoon or picture from a book, periodical, or newspaper;

II. *Multiple Copies for Classroom Use*

Multiple copies (not to exceed in any event more than one copy per pupil in a course) may be made by or for the teacher giving the course for classroom use or discussion; provided that:

A. The copying meets the tests of brevity and spontaneity as defined below; and,

B. Meets the cumulative effect test as defined below; and,

C. Each copy includes a notice of copyright.

Definitions

Brevity

(i) Poetry: (a) A complete poem if less than 250 words and if printed on not more than two pages or, (b) from a longer poem, an excerpt of not more than 250 words.

(ii) Prose: (a) Either a complete article, story or essay of less than 2,500 words, or (b) an excerpt from any prose work of not more than 1,000 words or 10% of the work, whichever is less, but in any event a minimum of 500 words.

[Each of the numerical limits stated in "i" and "ii" above may be expanded to permit the completion of an unfinished line of a poem or an unfinished prose paragraph.]

(iii) Illustration: One chart, graph, diagram, drawing, cartoon or picture per book or per periodical issue.

(iv) "Special" works: Certain works in poetry, prose or in poetic prose which often combine language with illustrations and which are intended sometimes for children and at other times for a more general audience fall short of 2,500 words in their entirety. Paragraph "ii" above notwithstanding such "special works" may not be reproduced in their entirety; however, an excerpt comprising not more than two of the published pages of such special work and containing not more than 10% of the words found in the text thereof, may be reproduced.

Spontaneity

(i) The copying is at the instance and inspiration of the individual teacher, and

(ii) The inspiration and decision to use the work and the moment of its use for maximum teaching effectiveness are so close in time that it would be unreasonable to expect a timely reply to a request for permission.

Cumulative Effect

(i) The copying of the material is for only one course in the school in which the copies are made.

(ii) Not more than one short poem, article, story, essay or two excerpts may be copied from the same author, nor more than three from the same collective work or periodical volume during one class term.

(iii) There shall not be more than nine instances of such multiple copying for one course during one class term.

[The limitations stated in "ii" and "iii" above shall not apply to current news periodicals and newspapers and current news sections of other periodicals.]

III. *Prohibitions as to I and II Above*

Notwithstanding any of the above, the following shall be prohibited:

A. Copying shall not be used to create or to replace or substitute for anthologies, compilations or collective works. Such replacement or substitution may occur whether copies of various works or excerpts therefrom are accumulated or reproduced and used separately.

B. There shall be no copying of or from works intended to be "consumable" in the course of study or of teaching. These include workbooks, exercises, standardized tests and test booklets and answer sheets and like consumable material.

C. Copying shall not:

(a) substitute for the purchase of books, publishers' reprints or periodicals;

(b) be directed by higher authority;

(c) be repeated with respect to the same item by the same teacher from term to term.

D. No charge shall be made to the student beyond the actual cost of the photocopying.

These guidelines are not intended to be a set of maximum standards but rather a set of minimum standards. If copying for classroom use stays within these guidelines, it will, without question, be considered fair use. It is conceivable that in a given case, a substantial departure from the guidelines might also be considered fair use, by application of the four basic statutory criteria.

Where an anticipated use falls outside the boundaries drawn by the guidelines, it is advisable to seek permission of the copyright owner. One way of doing this is to write directly to whoever is named in the copyright notice on the work. There will, of course, be works for which no copyright owner is clearly designated. For example, the copyright may be given in the name of a publisher that has gone out of business, or you may be working from a reprinted excerpt that does not bear copyright notice. In any case, unless it is appropriate to write to the publisher, you should write to the Copyright Office to request information regarding the copyright owners. If the Copyright Office is unable to provide guidance, it is likely that reproducing the work would be considered reasonable under the circumstances.

In general, publishers and authors are fairly accommodating in granting permission for educational uses of their works. However, that permission must be explicit. One is not entitled to rely on silence.

"Spontaneity" is a difficult quality to prove or disprove. However, your credibility will decrease, and your liability will increase, if the photocopying that you authorize begins to assume a pattern or if photo-copying is "spontaneously" authorized for works that ordinarily would be considered obvious parts of the curriculum.

The requirement that each copy reproduced for classroom use include a notice of copyright should be strictly complied with. Where you are taking an excerpt from a work in such a way that the copyright notice included in the work will not be reproduced, it is your responsibility to ensure that copyright notice in the proper form is put on each copy reproduced. This notice should be identical to that on the work itself. If you are reproducing a previously unpublished work—for example, a friend's manuscript—be certain to obtain his permission for publication. You should put proper notice on it, or a legend such as I have suggested for limited publications: "This copy is for private circulation only and may not be used in any other manner." To be safer yet, you might require each copy be returned to you at the end of the term.

The guidelines purport to cover single copying for a teacher's personal use. In my opinion they are prob-ably too narrow in this respect. However, copying for personal use must be distinguished from copying in the course of business, and "business" includes teaching duties.

It is important to remember that these guidelines expressly forbid the making of anthologies composed of periodicals and books, even though these may be sold to students at or below cost. They also forbid the copying of consumable items such as workbooks, standardized tests, and answer sheets. While some flexibility may exist in other part of the guidelines, it is doubtful that any court would sanction much de-viation in either of these respects.

Finally, these guidelines do not apply to sheet music, or to off-air taping of broadcasts. A teacher should seek administrative permission for any activity of this type.

Photocopying of Sheet Music for Classroom Use

With respect to sheet music, a compromise similar to that for literary works and works of art was made by the Music Publishers Association of the United States, Inc., the National Music Publishers Association, Inc., the Music Teachers National Association, the Music Educators National Conference, the National Association of Schools of Music, and the Ad Hoc Committee on Copyright Law Revision. The guidelines worked out by this group of organizations are as follows:[30]

A. *Permissible Uses*

1. Emergency copying to replace purchased copies which for any reason are not available for an imminent performance provided purchased replacement copies shall be substituted in due course.

2. (a) For academic purposes other than performance, multiple copies of excerpts of works may be made, provided that the excerpts do not comprise a part of the whole which would constitute a performable unit such as a section, movement or aria, but in no case more than 10% of the whole work. The number of copies shall not exceed one copy per pupil.

(b) For academic purposes other than performance, a single copy of an entire performable unit (section, movement, aria, etc.) that is [either] (1) confirmed by the copyright proprietor to be out of print or (2) unavailable except in a larger work, may be made by or for a teacher solely for the purpose of his or her scholarly research or in preparation to teach a class.

3. Printed copies which have been purchased may be edited or simplified provided that the fundamental character of the work is not distorted or the lyrics, if any, altered or lyrics added if none exist.

4. A single copy of recordings of performances by

students may be made for evaluation or rehearsal purposes and may be retained by the educational institution or individual teacher.

5. A single [phonorecord] of a sound recording . . . of copyrighted music may be made from sound recordings owned by an educational institution or an individual teacher for the purpose of constructing aural exercises or examinations and may be retained by the educational institution or individual teacher . . . [This guideline deals only with copyright in the music itself and not with copyright in the sound recording; the recording industry was not involved in negotiating these guidelines. However, I believe that the identical standard would apply to the sound recording copyright as well.]

B. *Prohibitions*

1. Copying to create or replace or substitute for anthologies, compilations or collective works.

2. Copying of or from works intended to be "consumable" in the course of study or of teaching such as workbooks, exercises, standardized tests and answer sheets and like material.

3. Copying for the purpose of performance, except as in A(1) above.

4. Copying for the purpose of substituting for the purchase of music, except as in A(1) and A(2) above.

5. Copying without inclusion of the copyright notice which appears on the printed copy.

Like the other photocopying guidelines, these are not intended to define the outer limits of fair use but to define minimum standards within which use may safely be assumed to be fair.

Guideline A(3) should not be understood to prohibit editing a piece of music in one's personal scholarly pursuits or as a classroom exercise. However, no teacher should make substantial revisions of a piece of music and distribute copies of the edited version or cause it to be performed, in class or elsewhere.

With respect to guideline A(4), no copyright owner's permission need be sought to sell recordings of student performances if the works performed have been previously recorded for public sale by someone else. The compulsory license for phonorecords would apply here.

The prohibition against the making of anthologies and the requirement that proper copyright notice be placed on each copy made for classroom use apply to sheet music just as to other printed works.

Copying of Computer Programs

None of the foregoing guidelines applies to copying of computer software. I am told that unauthorized copying of floppy disks is becoming a widespread practice in many schools. Any such copying is clearly beyond the bounds of fair use and should be avoided, unless of course the copies are strictly for archival purposes.

Classroom Performance or Display

It is permissible for teachers and their students to perform or display any work in class so long as the class is held on campus or, if off campus, in classroom-type circumstances and classroom-type surroundings. However, you cannot show a motion picture or other audiovisual work or display individual images from such a work if you know or suspect that the copy you use was not lawfully made.

Special Exemption: Institutions for the Deaf and Hearing Impaired

In the Conference Committee Report on the new statute, Congress adopted the view of Congressman Robert Kastenmeier, one of its leading copyright authorities, that fair use covers certain uses of television programs by nonprofit educational institutions for the deaf and hearing impaired. Congressman Kastenmeier had said that such an institution can make an off-the-air copy of a television program, make a captioned version of it, perform that version within the confines of the institution, and lend it to similar institutions for similar use. This use will be fair use only if it is noncommercial in every respect and if its purpose is to contribute to the student's learning environment.[31]

Library Copying

Among the issues of greatest concern in this area is that of copying for reserve use. Unfortunately Congress has not spoken on this matter. I believe that photocopying a chapter or similar small portion of a work for placement on reserve is a fair use, but this is no more than an informed guess.

The law does, however, specifically exempt from liability certain copying done in libraries.[32] (For convenience, I will use the word *library* to include archives.) The exemption is limited to circumstances in which the library making the copy owns the work as part of its own collection, only one copy is made, no charge is made for the copy beyond recovery of costs, and the copy made by the library bears the copyright notice that the work itself bears.

Subject to these limitations, it is permissible for a library to copy works under four circumstances:

1. If the work is unpublished and if a copy is necessary for purposes of preservation and security. To qualify under this exemption, the copy must be in "facsimile form." The meaning of this phrase is extremely broad; it includes, for example, microfilm; but it does not include putting a work into machine readable language for storage in an information system. What Congress had in mind when it made this distinction is unclear. A reasonable guess is that facsimile form is any form that stores the work in more or less its given medium. Microfilm qualifies because it reproduces the printed page; a computer data base does not because it stores a printed work by means of electromagnetic impulses.

2. If the work is unpublished and another library requests a copy for its own collection. Here, too, the copy must be in facsimile form.

3. If the work is published and the copy is needed to replace one that has been damaged, lost, or stolen, or is deteriorating. However, the library must first have made a reasonable effort to obtain an unused replacement at a fair price. The effort to find an unused replacement at a fair price would involve resorting to commonly known trade sources in the United States, to the publisher, and to any other copyright owner (if the owner can be located at the address listed in any copyright registration that has been made of the work). It will also involve checking with any central photocopying service that is authorized to reproduce the work. Certain additional efforts beyond these may be regarded as reasonable in a particular case but will be unnecessary in most cases. A copy made under this exemption must be a facsimile copy.

4. If the copy has been requested by a user of the library or by another library on behalf of one of its users. A copy made under this exemption must become the property of the user, and the library making the copy must have no reason to believe that it will be used for purposes other than private study, scholarship, or research. The exemption only applies if the library prominently displays a copyright warning notice at the place where patrons order copies, and on its order forms.[33] The form and placement of notice are prescribed by regulations, which are reproduced in appendix E. The exemption, moreover, is limited in subject matter; it does not apply to musical works, to pictorial or graphic works (except when used as illustrations of literary works), to sculptural works, or to motion pictures or other audiovisual works. Nor does it apply to any more than a small part of a work (meaning, in the

case of a periodical or other collective work, one solitary contribution), unless a copy of the work cannot be obtained at a fair price. To try to obtain a copy of the work, you must make an investigation. Furthermore, this exemption does not apply if the library is systematically distributing photocopies of copyrighted material, except where copies are not obtainable in the market at a fair price.

What is "systematic" copying? With respect to user requests, copying is probably systematic if it is available to any user with no questions asked. Copying done on a case-by-case basis only, with a clear requirement that there be some special need for it, will probably be all right. With respect to interlibrary arrangements, copying is systematic if it is so great or continuous as to substitute, in practical effect, for a purchase or subscription. The National Commission on New Technological Uses for Copyrighted Works (CONTU) has developed a set of specific guidelines to give flesh to this rather bare definition.[34] These guidelines, which have the unofficial blessing of Congress, may be summarized briefly here:

• With respect to periodical issues fewer than five years old, one library may obtain from another no more than five copies of material from any given periodical—as opposed to any given issue of a periodical—in any given calendar year.

• With respect to material other than periodicals, one library may obtain from another no more than five copies of or from any given work in any one calendar year.

• No guidelines are given for periodical issues published more than five years previous to the date of the request.

• If the requesting library has on order or in its collection the item that it wishes copied but does not have the item in its possession at the time, and cannot reasonably

repossess it at the time, the copy made at its request will not count toward the maximum number of permissible copies. For example, if a library has a book out at the binder, it can request a copy from another library without using up any of its five-copy allowance.
• A library cannot satisfy a request unless it is accompanied by a representation from the requesting library that the request conforms with these guidelines, if these guidelines apply.
• Every library must keep on file for three years each request it makes to another library.

None of these library exemptions applies if a library has reason to believe that its copying is, or is part of, a concerted reproduction of distribution of multiple copies of the same material. A "related and concerted" reproduction can take place over a period of time and need not involve one single user but can be with respect to a number of different users; it can also be found where a copy is requested by a group for the separate use of its various members.

None of the numerical restrictions on the library exemption appplies to videotape copies of news programs. A library may tape news broadcasts off the air and lend them to scholars and researchers for research purposes. Presumably it may also lend to other libraries for the same purposes. However, the term *news programs* is fairly narrow. It does not apply to documentaries (except "documentary programs involving news reporting"), or to magazine-format shows or other public-affairs broadcasts dealing with subjects of general interest.[35] For example, the special same-day reports prepared by the major networks on the abortive raid on Iran were "news programs"; segments of "Sixty Minutes" are not.

None of these exemptions either restricts or expands the rights of fair use. It is conceivable that in some cases the library would be safe in going beyond the limitations described here, if, in its considered judgment, the activity it contemplated was a fair use. On the other hand, the fact that a library may be exempt from liability in no way relieves an individual user who requests a copy from the library, if the making of that copy would not be a fair use. In short, these exemptions are for the benefit of the library and its personnel, not for persons making use of the library.

None of these exemptions overrules any contractual understanding a library may have with a copyright owner.

Finally, libraries are not liable for wrongful copying done on public machines if they have placed on the machines a warning against copyright infringement. (See appendix E.)[36]

So far I have dealt with the law that will apply to works created in 1978 or thereafter. In all respects but one, it is also the law that will apply to works created but neither published nor registered with the Copyright Office as unpublished works before 1978. (The previous federal statute permitted registration of certain works of the performing and visual arts prior to publication.) The one difference has to do with duration of the copyright term. The law makes a special provision for works in this category: no copyright for such a work can expire before December 31, 2002, and furthermore, if the work is published before that date, its copyright will not expire before December 31, 2027.

Works that were published or registered before 1978 are governed by a different set of rules. Although in many respects the new law will apply to those works, several fundamental provisions of the old system that have otherwise been discarded will also apply. Since these works are by far the majority of works in existence and will be for many years to come, it is important to know those portions of the old law that are still of concern.

Publication and Notice Under the Old Law

Chief among the basic premises of the old copyright system was the division between statutory copyright and common law copyright, a division based on the concept of publication. Common law copyright was, in essence, the right of "first publication"; it entitled its owner to exploit his work exclusively and in almost any manner for an unlimited period of time, so long as he did not publish it, and it entitled him to be the first to publish the work. Beyond that the common law would not go; once you published your work, you either assumed the mantle of federal statutory copyright, or, if you did not properly protect yourself, you forfeited your work to the public domain.

At the moment of first publication within the United States, notice became crucial. (Notice or lack of notice in foreign publication had no effect one way or the other.[1]) If you affixed proper notice to the work you automatically secured statutory copyright. If you failed to affix proper notice, your work went into the public domain.

Requirements for Notice under the Old Law

These requirements[2] were much the same as they are today, with certain important differences.

1. The date of first publication was not required on any copies except printed copies of literary, musical, or dramatic works, and phonorecords (called "reproductions" in the old law) of sound recordings.

2. On the first publication, only the name of the copyright proprietor could be used. Thus, on first publication the person whose name appeared in the notice had to be the owner of the entire copyright.

3. The full name of the copyright owner had to be used except on visual works and sound recordings; abbreviations, trademarks, and other symbols were not acceptable. If the name given in the notice on a visual work was in fact a trademark or other symbol, the full

and proper name had to appear somewhere, even if only on the bottom or back of the work.

4. Placement of the notice was strictly regulated. In the case of any printed work other than a periodical, notice had to be placed on the title page or the page immediately following. In the case of a periodical, it had to be placed on the title page or on the first page of text of each separate issue or under the title heading. In the case of sheet music or other printed musical work, it went on the title page or the first page of music. And in the case of phonorecords and visual works, it went in some "reasonable" place. ("Reasonable" had basically the same meaning as under the new law.)

5. Any defect in the notice, including omission of any part of proper notice, caused the work to be treated as if notice had been omitted entirely. There were only two exceptions. If, by accident or mistake, the year given in the notice was earlier than the true year of first publication, the copyright term simply began in the earlier year; and if, by accident or mistake, the year given was later than the true year by no more than a year, the fault was overlooked, at least where no innocent person, relying on the faulty notice, had begun to exploit the work thinking it to be in the public domain.[3] (This charitable approach to notices defective by only one year was a comparatively recent development.)

Under the old law, if notice was omitted or given improperly copyright was lost. There were not all the special indulgences provided in the new law for registration within five years, and so on; what was done could not be undone. There were only two exceptions. First, omission of proper notice had no effect if the copies or phonorecords were distributed without the authority of the copyright owner. Second, omission from a very small number of copies, if caused by accident or mistake (other than mistake as to what the law required), did not affect the copyright; however, an innocent person acting in the belief that the work was in the public domain (having been misled by the lack of notice) would not be liable for damages and could be enjoined from further infringement only if the copyright proprietor agreed to reimburse him for his out-of-pocket expenses.

Notice under the New Law for Works First Published Before 1978

The new law provides that works first published before 1978 may continue to abide by the old formalities of notice. Any new copies or phonorecords of those works can bear either the notice that was acceptable under the old law or that required by the new law. However, the reverse is not true. If copies or phonorecords distributed before 1978 did not carry notice that was proper at the time, the consequences will be governed by the old law, even though the notice might be permissible by post-1977 standards.[4]

Copyright Ownership under the Old Law

Indivisibility and the Periodicals Problem

The problem of notice brought into play another important principle of the old law, one which the new law has gone to great lengths to eliminate: that copyright ownership was indivisible. You could give other people licenses to use your work in one way or another, but you could not sell them any absolute right under the copyright; the only absolute transfer you could make was of the entire copyright as an undivided whole. This concept caused particular difficulties in the area of notice because the old statute specifically stated that notice at the time of first publication had to be in the name of the copyright owner or it would be considered to be no notice at all, and the work would go into the public domain. Thus if you gave a magazine permission to make first publication of a story but neither transferred copyright ownership to the magazine nor insisted that separate notice be inserted in your own name, copyright notice in the name of the magazine would not protect your copyright.

Over the course of time courts made many inroads in this rather rigid formalism, primarily by finding that an author had in fact conveyed all of his rights to the magazine, but that the magazine held them in trust for him, with a promise to reconvey them after publication. In 1970 the Second Circuit Court of Appeals (generally a bellwether court in copyright matters) simply abandoned the whole doctrine of indivisibility, at least so far as notice was concerned.[5] Thus if you made any sale or license of magazine rights after 1970, the chances are great, even though a court will be obliged to apply the old law to your case, that you will be protected by whatever notice was put on the magazine as a whole. Indeed, in most cases the Second Circuit's view could probably be applied to pre-1970 situations as well.

Presumably, this 1970 opinion swept away another old doctrine as applied to periodicals: that if a publisher, having secured copyright in its own name, conveyed its rights to someone else, the name in any copyright notice on the work could not be changed until the conveyance had been recorded with the Copyright Office.[6]

The same rules applied to derivative works and so-called composite works. (This term, roughly similar to the new term *collective works*, has vanished from the law as of 1978.) Movie rights contracts, for example, were often treated as licenses rather than sales, and so, theoretically, copyright notice in the name of the producer did not protect the copyright in any unpublished story licensed to the producer; fortunately, however, this problem seems to have surfaced very seldom in the movie context. Should a case come to trial now on a pre-1978 movie rights license, it is more than likely that a court will ignore the old doctrine of indivisibility and hold that notice in the name of the studio or the producer is not defective.

Another quirk of the indivisibility doctrine, and a particularly odd one, caused a great deal of mischief for many decades. This was the assumption that sale of an unpublished manuscript, painting, or other work, carried with it the sale of common law copyright in the work unless the seller expressed some clear intent to the contrary.[7] This rule was reversed by statute (at least as to works of fine art, though not as to manuscripts) in New York in 1966 and by statute in California in 1976.[8] ("Fine art" in the New York law meant paintings, sculpture, drawings, or graphic art. In California, it meant any kind of visual art.) It is not clear, however, what would happen if the case were to arise now concerning a sale carried out in either of those states before their laws were changed or in any state other than California and New York before 1978. Probably the old rule would be ignored, but I can offer no guarantee.

Works Made for Hire

The old law was much looser than the new law in its approach to works made for hire. Whether a work fell under the rule depended entirely on the intent of the persons involved. This meant that most commissioned works were regarded as works made for hire, but it meant also that an employer and employee could agree to waive the rule and could do so either orally or in writing.

There was some disagreement in the case of a commissioned work as to whether the commissioning party was to be treated as the author or only as the owner of the first term copyright. The latter view seems to be prevailing at the moment.[9] However, since the intent of the persons involved is a factor here as well, the question is open to litigation.

Whether a work was made for hire, and whether, in the case of a commissioned work, the hirer got the entire copyright or only the first term copyright, will be particularly important questions in the context of termination rights. They will also continue to affect the ownership of renewal rights.

Joint Works   In most respects, the old law governing joint works does not differ from the new law. However, the new law has rejected one doctrine that still has validity for pre-1978 works. This doctrine, first stated in what is known as the "12th Street Rag" case, is that intent to create a joint work can arise after one of the joint authors has already completed his part of the work.[10] Euday L. Bowman had composed "12th Street Rag" as an instrumental piano solo, and then assigned his rights to a publisher. The publisher commissioned lyrics for it. Bowman had had no notion of setting words to his music; it was entirely the publisher's idea; nonetheless, the court held that the resulting song was a joint work, giving the lyricist copyright in the music as well as the lyrics.

The court stressed that what mattered was the intent of whoever owned the copyright at the time the contributions were brought together, not the intent of either author at the time of creation. Effectively, it permitted someone to give up exclusive rights in a work by allowing it to be incorporated in a joint work. The doctrine would not extend, for example, to someone who sold movie rights in a novel to a producer, for in that case the seller does not intend that the novel will become merely a part of a movie.

Limited as it may be, this "12th Street Rag" doctrine will continue to affect royalty rights and renewal rights even under the new law, and will also have repercussions for termination rights under the new law. It should therefore be taken into account whenever you are dealing with a work which can be interpreted as a joint work.

Special Rules for Pre-1978 Sound Recordings and Phonorecords

Because under pre-1978 copyright law a thing from which a work could not be visually perceived was not an infringing "copy" of the work,[11] special rules arose concerning tapes and records, or what the new law calls phonorecords.

Until 1972 no protection at all was given by federal law to sound recordings. It was left to the states to pass record-piracy laws, and many of them did.[12] However, as of February 15, 1972, federal law was amended so as to apply to sound recordings published on or after that date. The new law largely carries this forward, with certain changes in the terms of the compulsory license. But pre-February 15, 1972, sound recordings will continue to be protected by state piracy laws until February 15, 2047, after which date they will be protected by federal law or not at all.[13]

What of the underlying musical works? Here there was great uncertainty. For years many courts believed that even though an unauthorized record or tape was not a copy that could infringe a musical work, issuing a record or tape of a musical work nonetheless published the work, and had to bear copyright notice covering the music. Many copyright lawyers disagreed, and advised composers who were their clients accordingly. As a result, many recordings were issued bearing no notice of copyright. Were the musical works put into the public domain? No one really knows.

In 1973 an authoritative opinion came down holding that if a record was not a copy for one purpose, it would not be a copy for another purpose.[14] But whether this eminently sensible decision clarified the law retroactively or only for the few remaining years of the old statute is not clear. My advice is to regard any musical work published in a pre-1973 recording as being still protected by copyright, regardless of whether it bears a copyright notice.

Copyright Term under the Old Law

The second major area in which the old law will continue to exert an influence for many decades to come is that of copyright duration, and particularly copyright renewal.

Under the old law, copyright lasted for a twenty-eight year term, but could obtain a second twenty-eight year term. Thus, for example, a copyright secured on May 12, 1932 would have run through May 11, 1960. If a copyright was not renewed in the last year of its first term, it went into the public domain. If it was renewed, it went into the public domain at the end of the second term. However, during the years that Congress was deliberating over the new statute, the expiration of second-term copyright was repeatedly postponed. Any work still in its renewal term on September 19, 1962 remained covered as of January 1, 1978.

Renewal of copyright was accomplished by filing an application for renewal with the Copyright Office in the last year of the original twenty-eight-year copyright term. Remember that if the notice on the work gave a date that was earlier than the true date of publication, the twenty-eight-year term ran from the date of notice, not from the date of first publication. This application could be filed by anyone, or on behalf of anyone, who was or might be entitled to the renewal term. In most cases, the person entitled had to be alive on the day that the renewal term was to begin or the renewal copyright would go to someone else. The right to renew was thus a mongrel sort of creation—rather like the termination right created by the new law—in that it was a right you possessed only so long as you lived.

If you were, say, a composer of music and had copyright in a musical score, you could file for renewal in the last year of your first copyright term. But if you died before that last year was up, the right to renew your copyright passed to your heirs or someone who had purchased the renewal copyright from you.

The provision for renewal, like that for termination under the new law, was designed to protect artists from themselves—and from the impossibility of knowing the true value of a work when it is first created—by giving them a chance to regain their copyrights after twenty-eight years. Unfortunately this noble purpose never was fulfilled, for those who wished to exploit artists, and those artists who preferred a dollar in hand to an uncertain hope of future riches, began to arrange sales and licenses of the renewal term in advance. (Generally these sales had to be explicit to be enforceable. A sale by an author of "all my right, title and interest" in a work was usually interpreted not to include a sale of the renewal copyright.)[15] Moreover, because the sale would be worthless if the artist died before having a chance to renew his copyright, it became common for spouses and children of artists to make ends meet by selling in advance whatever rights they might get if the artist died prematurely.[16]

Sales by authors and their families of the renewal term copyright have not always been upheld. If the seller can show that the sale was made under "such coercion of circumstances that enforcement would be unconscionable," a court will not enforce the bargain.[17] This is part of a growing tendency on the part of courts to invalidate unconscionable contracts of all kinds, and is not strictly a doctrine of copyright law.

Ownership of Copyright after Renewal

The basic rule was that copyright for the second term did not become anyone's property until the term actually began. At that point it became the property of whoever was by law entitled to renewal, but only if that person had actually applied for renewal (or if an application had been filed on his behalf). The validity of the application thus depended on the applicant's surviving until he became entitled to the copyright renewal. What made this provision particularly dangerous was that if the only person or persons who applied for renewal died before the commencement of the renewal term, the work would go into the public domain. To avoid this result, it became the general practice for everyone who might conceivably be entitled to file a claim for renewal to do so, just in case the author died prematurely.

The question of who was entitled to the renewal copyright was rather complicated. If an author died before the end of his first copyright term, the right to renew went to his surviving spouse and his children, or as many of them as were living, as a group. Any one of them, or all of them, could then apply for renewal, and when the renewal term began, the copyright would belong as of that moment to as many of the family as were alive at the time. (The surviving spouse retained the renewal right regardless of remarriage.)[18] For example, if a novelist died before renewal term began, leaving a husband and three children, any one of those four persons could apply for renewal, and to be safe, all four would apply. If all four were alive on the date that the renewal term began, each of them received a 25 per cent share in the new copyright. But if before that date one of those four died, the other three would take the second term's copyright in equal shares of one-third each. From that point on, the owners of the various shares were regarded as tenants in common. Each of them could make a transfer of the copyright but would have to account to the other owners for a fair share of the profits.

The law spoke only of children; more remote descendants were not mentioned. (Whether illegitimate children could take advantage of the statute used to depend on state law regarding the rights of illegitimate children, but it appears that illegitimate children can renew under the new law.)[19] The omission of more remote descendants meant that if the novelist in the example above died leaving no family except grandchildren, the renewal copyright would go to the executor of her estate, who would then pass it on to whoever was entitled to receive it by the terms of her will. If the novelist left no will, the copyright would go to her next of kin, who, in this case, would be the grandchildren. If, however, the novelist was survived only by her husband and her grandchildren, the husband would get the entire copyright and the grandchildren nothing. If she was survived by a child and by children of a deceased child, those grandchildren would not even take a *per stirpes* share. The rule seems harsh, but it has never been changed.

Because an application for renewal could be made "on behalf of" the person or corporation entitled to renewal, anyone who wished could apply for renewal, so long as he did so in the name of the person entitled by law to renew. For example, if the author had sold his right to the renewal term, he was still entitled by law to file the claim for renewal, but people who purchased the renewal copyright from an author rarely relied on the author to make the renewal claim; instead they filed the claim themselves on his behalf. Thus, also, a magazine contributor whose contribution had been registered only as part of a magazine issue could still apply for renewal, so long as he did so in the name of the owner of copyright in the magazine.[20] In this manner, he could protect his renewal copyright without having to depend on the publisher.

Renewal of Joint Works

In the case of a joint work, not all of the authors had to file for renewal since each of them had a right to treat the entire copyright as his own, although he had to account to his co-owners for any profits he made by doing so. This theory, if taken to its logical conclusion, ought to have meant that if only one of several joint authors obtained renewal of the copyright, he was the one who got the renewal term, subject to his obligation to account to his co-owners. However, the general rule has been to give all of the joint authors full ownership of the renewal term.[21]

Exceptions to These General Rules

There were four exceptions to the rule that an author or his surviving family, or his heirs, were entitled to the renewal copyright. For four categories of works, ownership of the original copyright brought with it entitlement to the renewal copyright as well.

The first category was that of so called posthumous works. What was a "posthumous work"? For a long time it was believed that a posthumous work was one not published before the author's death. However, though this definition fit in with familiar usage and conventional wisdom, it had the effect of disinheriting the author's spouse and children, for it meant that if an author before his death sold his copyright to someone else and died before publication, the purchaser would own the renewal right without having paid a dime for it. Responding to this clear inequity, the Second Circuit Court of Appeals in 1975 decreed that henceforth it would regard as posthumous only works in which the author had not, during his life, made any contract for exploitation of his copyright by publication, performance, or otherwise.[22] This meant that the only person who would have the right to renew copyright in a posthumous work would be the person who inherited the copyright from the author. That, of course, still left it open to the author to bequeath his common law copyright by will to some unrelated person, but the practical effect of the new rule has generally been a tremendous benefit to the families of authors. This definition of posthumous works has been adopted by Congress for all renewals made after January 1, 1978.[23]

The second category was of works published without separate notice in a magazine or other "composite work." The author of the contribution did not possess the renewal right unless his work bore a separate copyright notice.[24] However, the practical significance of this was minimal, because if the publisher held the original copyright in trust for the author, as courts have recently tended to declare, it would also hold the renewal copyright in trust.

The third and fourth categories, unlike the first two categories, were not flexible. The third comprised all works made for hire. This was of particular significance considering the wide range of works that could be considered works made for hire. The fourth comprised works in which copyright originally belonged to a corporate body (for example, a company, a board of trustees, or a charitable society). Since this would not be so if the corporate body was not itself the author of the work, in most cases this fourth exception simply overlapped with the work made for hire exception.

Renewal under the New Law

Any pre-1978 work must be renewed in exactly the same way, and to the benefit of exactly the same persons, as it would have been under the old law. There is a new and different renewal application form (form RE), and the fee for renewal has gone up to $6, but otherwise the old law carries over, with only a few substantial changes.[25]

Renewing a Group of Works

As I have mentioned above, under the new law it is possible for an author to register a number of contributions to collective works on the same form. The new law has a similar provision where renewal is concerned. In the case of the works of an individual author, renewal registration may be made on a single form and for a single fee if these conditions are met:

• If the renewal claimant or claimants are the same for each work. For example, if a magazine owns two of the renewal rights and the author's family own the other two, the same registration form cannot be used for all four works.

• If the basis of the claim is the same for each work. This will be the case in all but a very few circumstances. An example to the contrary would be if the publisher is entitled to renew some works because their renewal terms were assigned to it by the author and entitled to renew others because they were works made for hire; in both cases the publisher is the proper renewal claimant, but it cannot use the same form to renew all of these works.

• If the works were all copyrighted at the time of their first publication, either by separate notice and registration or by virtue of a copyright notice having been affixed to the periodical issue as a whole, regardless of whether that issue was registered.

• If all the works were published in one calendar year.

• If the application identifies each work, and states the name and date of the periodical issue in which it was first published.[26]

Length of Renewal Term

The new law has lengthened the renewal term for pre-1978 works.[27] It might seem unfair that authors of works copyrighted before 1978 should not get the benefit of the life-plus-fifty term, but Congress felt that altering the structure of existing copyrights to that extent would upset the financial expectations of people who had invested in them and would cause numerous other difficulties and contradictions. Instead Congress added nineteen years to the renewal term of copyright for works in their first term as of January 1, 1978. Those works, if renewed, are now protected for a total of seventy-five years from the year of first publication.

The renewal term for works that were already in their second term when the new law went into effect, or for which a timely renewal application was still pending on December 31, 1977, has also been lengthened by nineteen years. Those works, too, will thus be protected for a total of seventy-five years from the year of first publication.

In all cases, the copyright term for pre-1978 works that were still under copyright on January 1, 1978, runs through the end of the calendar year in which it would otherwise expire. This is a great improvement over prior law.

The addition of nineteen years is intended to benefit authors, not the people to whom they may have sold their rights. To ensure that this will in fact be the result, the new law has adopted a procedure for terminating renewal term grants, and that includes not only grants of the renewal right but also any grant or license that applies to the renewal term. The procedure is similar in most respects to that for terminating transfers of post-1977 copyrights.

Terminating Pre-1978 Grants of Renewal Rights

The right to terminate transfers of renewal copyright[28] applies only to transfers made before January 1, 1978 of copyright in works published before that date. No grant or license concerning the renewal term made after December 31, 1977 can be terminated. The right is not available for works made for hire, and it does not affect grants made by will or grants of rights in foreign countries. Furthermore, it only affects the nineteen-year extension period, not the basic twenty-eight-year renewal term.

Grants Made by Persons Other than the Author

It is now possible for an author's spouse or children to terminate grants of renewal rights that they have made. It is also possible for them to terminate any grant that takes effect during the renewal term.

Termination must be made by all of the grantors who are still alive. Thus if three children joined in making a grant of renewal rights and two of them die, the remaining child can effect termination all by himself. But if all three children are still alive, all three must join in making the termination.

The heirs of a deceased grantor other than the author have no termination rights. Thus, in my example, if two children die before having a chance to take part in the termination, the remaining child is the only person who can effect termination; a deceased child's children have no rights in this respect. Nor do they have any rights once termination has been carried out. However, from the moment that the copyright reverts to the persons who terminated the grant, which it does on the date the termination becomes effective, it becomes property; it is no longer personal to the grantor but can be inherited. Thus if a child dies after taking part in the termination, his heirs will get an equal share of the copyright. This distinction seems unfair, but it is nonetheless the law.

Grants Made by the Author

Termination of grants of renewal rights made by the author may be made by him alone, if he is living. If the author is dead, the termination right is owned and may be exercised by his family. His spouse has the entire right if there are no children or grandchildren; his children and grandchildren have the entire right if there is no spouse; if there are both a spouse and children or grandchildren, the spouse has half the termination right and the children and grandchildren have the other half, divided among them in equal shares *per stirpes*. The share of a deceased child can be exercised only by a majority of his children. In short, apportionment of the termination rights is identical to that provided for grants of copyright in post-1977 works.

Grants of Renewal in Joint Works

Any author who joined in a grant of rights regarding the renewal term may terminate the grant to the extent of his share of the rights. (If he is dead, his termination right may be exercised by his family.) This provision for joint works differs substantially from the rule covering grants of copyright in post-1977 works. The rule in the latter case is that a majority of authors who signed the original grant must join in giving notice of termination; but in the case of grants concerning the renewal term made before January 1, 1978, each of the joint authors can terminate his own individual share of the grant. This may work some hardship in years to come, for it appears that if one of the joint owners pulls out, he can make a grant to someone else, and the person who has the original grant will be stuck paying royalties to the other joint authors but without any longer having an exclusive license.

Ownership of Copyright after Termination of a Grant Made by the Author

When a grant made by an author is terminated, the copyright reverts on the date termination becomes effective. However, it does not necessarily revert to the persons who made the termination, as is the case for grants made by someone other than the author. The reversion goes to the author or, if he is deceased, to his family, in the same proportions as the termination rights, but without regard to who signed or did not sign the termination notice. For example, a child who did not sign the termination notice still receives a proportionate share of the copyright when it reverts.

Any new grant of a right that has reverted in this manner is valid only if it is in writing, and only if it is signed by the same number of persons, and by persons representing the same proportion of ownership, as were required to carry out termination. This is so whether the new grant is exclusive or nonexclusive. (A new grant of a right originally granted by persons other than the author does not have to meet these "number" and "proportion" requirements.)

An example may help to demonstrate these rules. Suppose that termination rights in a work are owned 50 per cent by the author's widow and 25 per cent by each of two daughters. Termination would have to be carried out by at least two persons (the widow and at least one daughter). At the time of notice, the right to reversion of the copyright vests in the widow and daughters in the same proportions. Suppose that one of the daughters then dies, leaving her share of the copyright to her alma mater. (She was able to make this bequest because ownership of the copyright had vested in her.) In order for a new grant of the copyright to be valid, it must be signed by at least two persons, who must represent at least the same percentage of the right as was required for termination. But they need not be the same persons who terminated the original grant. Thus the statute is satisfied if the grant is signed by the widow and the college.

The new grant binds and benefits even those who did not participate in it. Thus, the daughter who does not sign the new grant is still legally bound by it, and the buyer is obligated to pay her a share of the royalties.

Mechanics for Terminating a Renewal Term Grant

The following rules apply to all terminations of renewal right grants, whether the grants were made by the author or by his family.[29]

1. Termination may take effect at any time during the five-year period beginning either fifty-six years from the date that copyright in the work was first secured, or January 1, 1978, whichever date is later.

2. Notice of termination, which must be in writing and signed by all persons whose consent is required for termination, must be given not more than ten years and not fewer than two years before the date that termination is to take effect.

3. A copy of the notice must be recorded in the Copyright Office before the date of termination, or the termination is null and void. The fee for recording is $10, plus $.50 for every page over six.

4. As with the termination of grants of post-1977 copyrights, no new grant, and no agreement to make a new grant, can be made until the date termination becomes effective, except that renegotiation of an existing grant may be made as soon as notice is given. Rights under a renegotiated contract do not ripen until termination takes effect.

A notice of termination must contain certain basic information:

1. The name of the persons whose rights are being terminated and the address to which the notice is being sent. If you are sending notice to more than one address, list all of them.

2. The title of the work.

3. The name of at least one author of the work.

4. The date that copyright was secured.

5. The copyright registration number, if possible.

6. The exact nature of the grant you are terminating.

7. The date that termination is to become effective.

8. If the grant was made by someone other than the author, a list of all persons who made the original grant and who are still alive.

9. If the grant was made by the author but is being terminated by his family, a list of all the persons who are entitled to take part in termination (whether they are actually doing so or not) and their relationships to the author. Indicate on the list which persons actually are taking part in the termination and what their percentage shares of the termination right are.

If you are not sure of all this information, put down as much as you know and explain why you are uncertain as to the rest.

The notice must be signed by all persons taking part. Each signature should be accompanied by the person's name and address, in legible form. The notice must also contain a statement that to the best of their knowledge those persons have, among them, a sufficiently large share of the termination right to entitle them to terminate.

The notice must be delivered by hand or by first-class mail. It is your duty to make reasonably sure that the person to whom you are giving the notice is still the owner of the right and has not granted it to someone else, and also that you have the correct address. This means that you should write to the Copyright Office and request a search for recordations of any transfers. (This will probably incur a small fee.) In the case of musical works, you should also check with ASCAP or one of other performing-rights societies.

If you fail to comply with any of these requirements and if your errors or omissions cause other people to be misled in some harmful way, your notice of termination may be judged legally ineffective.

Effect of These Rules on Derivative Works

Because expiration of copyright in an underlying work throws substantial portions of a derivative work into the public domain, it has been common practice for movie producers, for example, to make sure that copyright in the novels they use for their plots is renewed. This will continue to be valid practice.

On the other hand, termination of a renewal term grant to make a motion picture, for example, will not prevent any film already made from being exploited. It will only prevent the producer from making a new film of the same story.

Tax Treatment of Copyrights

Authors generally have two tax problems: how to report their income and how to deduct their expenses. Other copyright owners have similar problems but from a different perspective. For them, the problems are not much different from those of someone who buys a machine or farm. For an author, though, Congress has created a veritable funhouse of rules.

The Author as Owner: When Is an Asset Not an Asset?

The author's trouble arises principally from governmental ambivalence as to whether a copyright is a capital asset in the hands of its creator. The decision was made many years ago to deny authors long-term capital gain treatment for the sale of their copyrights.* Thus an author is like someone who builds houses rather than like someone who buys them: his profit is taxed as ordinary income. Nonetheless, if he is a professional author, he must treat some of his expenses as capital investments, and if he is not he must treat

*For purposes of this chapter, when I use the term capital gain I mean long-term capital gain. Strictly speaking, there is also short-term capital gain (i.e., gain on sales of capital assets held less than a year), which is taxed like ordinary income. However, since most laymen (and many lawyers, myself included) tend to ignore this in ordinary speech, I will follow suit.

them all as capital investments. When and how those expenses can later be deducted also depends on whether the author is a professional.

As you can see, this is not an area where common sense or logic will necessarily be of help. The thing to have is a map and a rulebook, and I hope what follows will serve.

The Amateur   An amateur author cannot deduct any of the expenses of his hobby unless and until he sells the work.[1] An amateur author is one who is not engaged in the trade or business of creating copyrighted works. For example, someone who paints for recreation is an amateur for tax purposes, however good the paintings may be.

The question that decides whether someone is an amateur or a professional is whether the activity is carried on primarily for livelihood or profit or primarily for recreation. Dim hopes of future glory will not convert a hobby into a trade. On the other hand, financial failure does not brand one as an amateur, if one has made a genuine effort to sell one's creations.[2] Nor is it necessary that the activity be one's sole pursuit in life: painting on weekends may still be a profession if you are actively trying to sell the results.

The regularity with which you pursue an activity will help determine whether you are a professional or an amateur.[3] The tortoise is more professional than the hare.

The   Generally, if you are a professional author, costs relating
Professional   to your title in a copyright cannot be deducted in the year you incur them. Instead they have to be capitalized—that is, treated as investments—and depreciated over the useful life of a copyright. Other expenses, such as travel, secretarial help or the cost of supplies, may

be deducted in the year they are incurred. The basic principles are these:

Costs Relating to Title   This phrase covers the cost of copyright registration, including legal fees. It also covers all expenses, including legal fees, you may incur in defending your copyright against someone who accuses you of infringing or in suing an infringer yourself. However, it does not include expenses incurred or damages won in defending or asserting a right to income. By the same token, damages that are in the form of profits are taxed as ordinary income. Damages that relate to title are not taxable as income but the amount of them must be subtracted from the capital basis on which you compute depreciation.

This is the sort of hairsplitting that has earned the Internal Revenue Code a bad name. Suppose you become involved in a complicated infringement suit, where not only the basic title to copyright but also the right to royalties is at stake. How do you decide where title ends and right to royalties begins? The best you can do is to ask the court to apportion the damages it awards you between the two and apply the same ratio to your legal costs and to the damages you win. Sometimes your attorney will be able to give you an itemized bill, but this method of allocating legal costs runs a greater risk of being overruled by the IRS.

The foregoing applies only if you win. If the court decides your claimed copyright is invalid and you lose, all of your expenses will be deductible in the year the decision is handed down, and you will also be able to deduct the dollar value of the title you have lost (but not the value of projected income) in the year the decision is handed down. Expenses that arise from litigation over income will be deductible when paid.

Other Expenses   The law permits you to deduct your outlay for supplies, secretarial help, travel, research, and other expenses. For example, if you travel to another country to do background research for a book, you may deduct the cost of travel as a cost of doing business. If you hire someone to do the research, the same rule applies.[4]

Depreciation   The tax laws permit an author to take a deduction each year for a portion of the capital value of a copyright, until it is reduced almost to zero. Depreciation should be taken over the useful life of the copyright. The presumption is that copyright will retain its value for its entire duration: life plus fifty years, or whatever the applicable term is. However, if you can prove that your copyright has a market life of only a few years, you can speed up your depreciation. Thus if you have written a textbook with a predictable market life of only six years, you can deduct one-sixth of your capital costs in each of those six years, starting with the year of first publication.[5] The general rule for depreciation is that it cannot begin until the asset is "placed in service." With works that are not published but are exploited by performance or display, depreciation would begin when exploitation begins. An interesting question, to which no one has the answer, is whether an unpublished work is "placed in sevice" when derivative works based upon it are published. I tend to think it is.

I use the phrase "almost to zero" because until you dispose of your copyright you cannot depreciate it below what is termed "salvage value."[6] Salvage value is, basically, what you could get for the copyright, even after income has dwindled away, by selling it to some optimistic buyer who hopes for a backswing in the pendulum of public taste or who wants to be able to use parts of your work without threat of suit. In most cases salvage value will be negligible. If your copyright is valuable, though, salvage value may be a factor, and you should consult your tax advisor on this point.

Matching Depreciation to Income

If you sell your copyright for a flat fee, you can deduct the remaining balance of your capital value in the year of sale. However, if you sell on a royalty basis, you should take your depreciation deductions against royalty income. In such a case, the rules differ depending upon whether you can predict your income flow. If you can, you should adjust your depreciation accordingly. For example, if you can predict that income will be $20,000 in the first year, $10,000 in the second year, $5,000 in the third, and zero in the fourth, for a total of $35,000, you can deduct twenty thirty-fifths of your capital value in the first year, ten thirty-fifths in the second, and the remaining five thirty-fifths in the third (always, of course, allowing for salvage value).[7] If you cannot predict your income flow, you can deduct for depreciation in any given year up to the amount of income you receive.[8]

Deduction for Loss

If you abandon or forfeit your copyright, if it is taken away from you in a lawsuit, or if it becomes valueless, you can deduct the remaining balance of your capital value in the year the loss occurs.[9]

Special Problems for Sculpture, Paintings, and Plates

This discussion has so far dealt with the copyright itself, an intangible property right. A sculptor or painter, however, produces something tangible as well, quite apart from the copyright in the work. So does a printmaker or photographer. So, too, does a publisher.

The physical object has a value quite separate from that of the copyright. It is a capital-type asset. Because of this, the costs of the materials and so on that go into it must be capitalized, even though they might otherwise be regarded as business expenses. Sometimes this will lead to allocation problems. For example, if you are a welder in steel, what part of your electricity costs has to be attributed to the object? Your guess is probably as good as the IRS's so long as you guess in good faith. Depreciation cannot be taken unless the object is likely to deteriorate noticeably in the owner's lifetime. Sale of the object by the author will produce ordinary income.

Joint Authors

Where there are two or more joint authors, the depreciation basis must be divided among them in the same proportions as their ownership. Unless there is an agreement to the contrary, each joint author will take an equal share of the basis.

Gift and Estate Taxes

The irony is that when an author makes a private gift of a copyright, it is valued for gift tax purposes at its fair market value. It may have a basis of only $200, but if its market value (based on projected income) is $20,000, the author is treated as making a gift of $20,000. Yet a gift to charity will not be valued at fair market value, but at the author's capital value.

Whether a gift other than to charity will actually incur gift tax depends upon the number of donees, whether the author's spouse joins in making the gift, and whether the author has used up his "unified credit against gift and estate taxes." These are complex questions and outside the scope of this book. If you are making a gift to any one person of a copyright with a probable market value of over $10,000—the limit on tax-free gifts in any given year—you should consult a tax advisor.

A gift of a royalty interest will not circumvent this rule. Indeed, a gift of a royalty interest, without any transfer of ownership or of contract rights in a work, will not even suffice to make the income taxable to the donee rather than the author, although it will nonetheless be taxed as a gift.[10]

A copyright is valued in the author's estate at its market value, no matter whether it is left to a private person or to charity. Thus if a copyright is left to charity, the estate receives a deduction for its full market value.

To add to the confusion, one who receives a copyright by gift takes the author's own basis, whereas one who receives it by inheritance is able to take the estate tax value.

Special Rules for Corporations

Copyright in a film or other work produced by a large corporation, whose creative staff are paid a salary and have no financial stake in the corporation, in many cases can be treated as a capital asset if the corporation is in the trade or business of exploiting it rather than of selling or brokering it.[11]

Special Rules for Movies

In general, production of copyrighted works is not eligible for the so-called investment tax credit. However, in 1976 an exception was made for movies and videotapes created primarily for entertainment or educational purposes. The computation of this credit is exceedingly complex. If you have produced a movie or videotape of this type, you should consult a lawyer or accountant for specific advice.

Copyright as Capital Asset: Persons Other Than the Author

A different set of rules applies to a person to whom the author gives, bequeaths, or sells his copyright. The basis for such a person depends on which type of transfer occurs.

Basis in an Acquired Copyright

Donees

Basis in a gift is determined by looking at what lawyers call the owner's "chain of title." If you obtain a copyright by gift, your basis depends on who gave it to you. If you got it from the author, your basis is the author's basis, less any depreciation already taken before it reaches you. The same is true if you got it from someone who was given it by the author. There can be any number of gifts, but if the chain began with the author, the author's basis (as adjusted along the way) will be the basis for every owner in the chain. However, if someone in the chain of title purchased or inherited the copyright, the basis you get is that purchase price, or the estate value, less any depreciation taken on it since then. Each purchase or inheritance in a chain of title sets a new basis for the copyright.

Inheritors

The tax laws give a break to someone who receives a copyright by inheritance. Basis is "stepped up"to the value of the copyright in the author's estate. Admittedly this makes a strange distinction between, say, a child of an author who is given a copyright and a child who gets it by inheritance. Recently there was an effort to eliminate this distinction, not by being kinder to the first child, but by denying any benefit to the second. For a short time there was on the books a new law, establishing what was called "carryover basis," which would have required an inheritor of a copyright (or any other kind of property, for that matter) to take the decedent's basis. Fortunately, this law has been repealed.

Purchasers

If you purchase a copyright, your basis will be what you paid for it. However, for there to have been a purchase, there has to have been a sale. The term *sale*, as used in the tax laws, has a special meaning. Because a copyright is a bundle of distinct rights, there can be a sale of one of those rights even if the others are retained. For example, you can have a sale of the publication right alone. However, if the transferor retains too much control over the right, there is no sale even though, for purposes of the copyright law, there has been an exclusive transfer.

The only controls that it is certain a seller can safely retain are the right to sue for infringement and the right to rescind the transfer for failure to make royalty payments or because the transferee has gone bankrupt (although current bankruptcy law nullifies any such right), or because the transferee fails to market the property. The general principle here is that a transfer is a sale so long as rescission can occur only because of some event that is not in the seller's control.[12] The statutory right to terminate a transfer does not affect the status of a "sale."

A transfer may be limited in geographical scope. If it is, it should be paid for not on a royalty basis but in a lump sum, or it will be treated as a license and not a sale. Conversely, if paid for on a royalty basis it will be considered a sale only if the exclusive rights given are without geographical limitation.[13] And all of this is without regard to whether the arrangement would be called a transfer of ownership for copyright purposes such as recordation.

In many cases, a purchaser will want to have a transfer characterized as a license so that he can deduct his payments as a cost of doing business instead of capitalizing them. The seller is just as likely to want the opposite. When the transaction is ambiguous, this will be an important bargaining point for both sides.

Depreciation

A donee or inheritor of a copyright can take depreciation only if a copyright is producing income. A purchaser of a copyright, assuming that the purchaser has acquired the property for investment purposes and not as a broker or trader in copyrights, can take depreciation regardless of whether income is being received. A broker or trader in copyrights holds the copyrights as inventory and cannot take depreciation at all.

The depreciation rules for someone who receives a copyright by gift or inheritance are generally the same as for an author: depreciation may be taken against income in any of the ways discussed. A purchaser of a copyright must also follow these rules if he holds the copyright for investment purposes, except that he can take a deduction in a year of no income. All three types of persons can take a deduction for loss or forfeiture.

Capital Gain Treatment

Any holder of a copyright other than the author or one who takes the author's basis is entitled to treat the sale of a copyright as capital gain, provided that he has held the copyright for over a year. (The one-year holding period is not required for inheritors of copyright.)[14] This treatment is available only if there is a sale within the meaning of the tax laws. If the tax laws treat the disposition as a license, then receipts must be treated as ordinary income.

11 International Copyright Protection and the Manufacturing Clause

If you know something of the life of Charles Dickens, you know something also of the chaos that existed in the early days of bulk printing, when, in the view of the U.S. Government, copyrights stopped at the borders of an author's native land. Dickens and other popular English writers suffered wholesale piracy of their works by American printers, until at last the U.S. Senate, against strong domestic pressure, agreed by treaty to recognize English copyrights.

Copyright is, intrinsically, a creature of national law. However, there are now few countries that do not have treaty arrangements for the international protection of copyrights. Most of these countries are members of either or both of the two great conventions, as they are called: the Berne Convention, and the Universal Copyright Convention. These conventions are essentially multilateral agreements to give certain recognition to copyrights that arise in other member countries. Neither of these conventions requires a member nation to protect copyright in sound recordings. There is a separate treaty on this subject, the Convention for the Protection of Producers of Phonograms Against Unauthorized Duplication of Their Phonograms. However, the membership of this convention is comparatively small.

The United States belongs to the UCC but not to the Berne Convention. The new copyright law was enacted partly in the hope that its terms would qualify the United States for membership in Berne, but so far that has proved illusory. Like the United States, most Berne countries give protection for the life of the author plus fifty years. However, Berne countries have no notice requirements, and it is this factor, principally, that stands in the way of our joining that convention.

Probably, though, U.S. copyrights obtain almost all the important protection they need from the UCC; it was, in fact, largely an American idea. Although it was formed when the old law was still in effect, it appears to work equally well under the new law.

For published works the UCC provides that every member nation will give to a work first published in another member nation, or created by a citizen of another member nation, the same protection that it gives works of its own citizens that are first published within its own borders. For example, Japan must give works of U.S. authors the same protection that it gives to Japanese works that are first published in Japan. (However, this is qualified somewhat in the case of copyright duration.)

For unpublished works every member nation must protect the works of citizens of other member nations, just as it protects those of its own citizens.

There are, nonetheless, certain minimum standards of protection that a member nation must extend to foreign works, even if it does not extend them to works of its own citizens or works first published within its borders.

1. The copyright term must be at least the life of the author plus twenty-five years or twenty-five years from publication or registration. This minimum term is not required for photographic works and works of applied

art in member nations that do not grant copyright to such works by their own citizens, but if a member nation does grant copyright to such works, it must grant at least a ten-year term. A more sweeping exception to the minimum term is that if a work belongs to a class of works that is protected for a shorter term—which, in the extreme case, would be no term at all—in the country of origin, then a member nation has no obligation to grant it a longer term of protection. (The country of origin is the country of first publication, or, in the case of an unpublished work, the country of which the author is a citizen.) For example, because buildings are not protected by copyright in the United States, France has no obligation to protect the design of an American building against infringement in France, even though it does protect the designs of French buildings.[1] This rule is discretionary with the governments involved. Denmark, West Germany, Japan, the Netherlands, Sweden, Finland, Israel, France, Italy, and the Vatican all follow it to varying degrees; the first five countries apply it only where the term of the foreign work is shorter, not where there is no term at all.[2]

2. A member nation cannot impose its own formalities on foreign works as a condition of copyright. The one exception is the formality of renewal term applications. All other formalities—such as notice, registration, and recordation—will be considered satisfied if from the time of first publication all copies of the work published with the authority of the copyright proprietor bears notice in this form: © name of proprietor, year of first publication. (The copyright proprietor is the person who owns the basic underlying copyright.) This notice must be placed so as to give reasonable notice of the copyright claim.[3]

3. Every member nation must protect the author's exclusive translation right; however, it may require the

author to license that right if no translation has been published in any of its languages within seven years of first publication.[4]

4. Every member nation must protect the author against unauthorized reproduction of any kind. This provision was adopted in 1971 and was aimed especially at photocopying and other new reproduction technologies. This and the translation right are subject to certain special exceptions in developing countries.[5]

5. Every member nation must protect the author's exclusive performance and broadcasting rights.

This is the theoretical framework. The practical question is, What do you have to do to get the benefits of the UCC? The answer is that so long as your work is unpublished, there is nothing at all you can or need do. If you are a U.S. citizen or a citizen of another UCC country, protection is automatic. Once you publish, assuming you publish first in the United States, you must follow the U.S. rules; no country has stricter formalities than the United States, and U.S. notice will protect your rights everywhere. Many countries do not require notice at all, but if you intend to market your book in a foreign country you should use the UCC form of notice, which is acceptable domestically as well.

A word should be said here about the old U.S. publishing custom of carrying out so-called simultaneous publication in Canada or England (both Berne Convention countries) so as to get the benefit of Berne rules. Simultaneous publication has always been something of a comedy. It was often achieved by leaving a couple of copies in a Canadian warehouse and advertising in the local papers that they were for sale. As an alternative, one sometimes took affirmative steps. I once arranged Canadian publication for a client by having a friend in Ontario take copies to two friends of his.

The virtues of this charade are doubtful. Prior to 1978, one achieved a longer copyright term in the Berne countries by doing it. That incentive is now gone. My own endeavor was post-1977, but it was for the purpose of securing protection in those few Berne countries that are not members of the UCC. In most cases, this would not be much of a gain; the countries involved are ones that rarely represent major markets.

Moreover, it is not all clear that simultaneous publication is effective. Canadian law forbids the importation of a book until two weeks after it has been first published in another country. This law has never been enforced, but it does exist. Moreover, some Berne countries refuse to recognize a Canadian or U.K. first publication unless it is exclusive.[6] All things considered, you would be wise to avoid getting entangled in this sort of operation unless it is absolutely necessary.

When Congress adopted universal copyright protection, it did not, unfortunately, put aside all nationalism. That spirit lingers on in chapter 6 of the Copyright Act, commonly referred to as the "manufacturing clause."

In essence, the manufacturing clause forbids the import into this country, and public distribution within this country, of more than 2,000 copies of any work not "manufactured" here or in Canada, if it is made up preponderantly of nondramatic literary material in the English language. This provision is a good deal narrower than the corresponding provision of the previous copyright statute. How it came to survive the transition at all, and then to be extended for another four years beyond the July 1, 1982 expiration date originally enacted, is an uninspiring lesson in politics. There is little or no evidence that the protection it offers to domestic printers and binders is needed. But as someone has said, those who love sausage and respect the law should never watch either of them being made.

In general, the manufacturing clause does not apply if any substantial part of the English language material is the work of an author who is neither a citizen of nor domiciled in the United States, or who is a U.S. citizen but who has been living outside the United States for at least a year prior to importation or distribution. Thus, for example, if a work is a joint work and one of the authors is a French citizen living in France, the manufacturing clause does not apply to the work. The rules are somewhat tighter in the case of a work made for hire; no employer/author of any substantial part of the work may be a U.S. citizen (no matter where he or she is living), or be living in the United States, or be a U.S. domestic business. However, regardless of the author's citizenship or whereabouts, the manufacturing clause does not apply if the work was first published outside the United States by a foreign publisher and has not been published in any authorized U.S. edition, so long as the author is an individual and is receiving compensation for the U.S. distribution, and the copies imported have been manufactured outside the United States under license directly from the author or from the foreign publisher.

Manufacture, as used in the statute, includes typesetting or the making of plates from type, if the printing is done directly from the plates or set type; platemaking, if the plates that are used in reproducing the work are made by a lithographic or photoengraving process; and in any event, printing and binding. All of these functions, unless the work is in braille, must be performed in the United States or Canada or the quotas will apply. Interestingly, the statute is specifically designed to perpetuate a loophole of which some U.S. publishers have long taken advantage, and that is the making of plates in this country from "reproduction proofs" made from type set overseas. The statute would also permit publishers to import computer tapes made overseas, so long as the plates made from the printout were manufactured here.[7]

You need not fear that customs agents will seize books from your suitcase at Kennedy Airport. An exemption is given for copies brought into the country by individuals as part of their personal baggage. Also, you are free to have single copies imported directly to you. Furthermore, religious, scholarly, and educational institutions can import copies for their libraries, and governmental bodies can import copies for their use other than in schools. Copies that are brought in under any of these exemptions do not count toward the 2,000 limit for import or public distribution.

If you are planning to import copies of any work that comes within the purview of the manufacturing clause and do not qualify for any of the special exemptions, you should obtain from the Copyright Office an "import statement" to present to U.S. Customs. This can be obtained upon request once the work has been registered.

The practical effect of failure to comply with the manufacturing clause is that any infringer of your publication right who has had his copies manufactured here or in Canada has a complete defense to a lawsuit. He cannot with impunity infringe any other rights in the work, such as the right of performance, but he can publish to his heart's content. The only way you can put a stop to his activities is by bringing out an edition of the work that has been manufactured here or in Canada, and registering it with the Copyright Office.[8]

Afterword

Information is power, as we are often told. But like most other kinds of power, it has no value except in use. We as a society benefit from that use and so we encourage authors as best we know how, realizing, as Samuel Johnson once put it, that "nobody but a blockhead ever wrote except for money."

However, as international copyright law demonstrates, people outside the free-market democracies do not view this equation in the same way. Our economies require raw materials; what the economies of developing countries require from us above all else, more than consumer goods and fancy weapons and the other vanities of modern life, is information. If they are to modernize, they must have access to our technical and scientific literature. In many cases, these countries have agreed to pay for it only after receiving substantial concessions.

The international copyright system works reasonably well at the moment. But there are difficulties ahead. As computer software increases the sophistication of our technology, the gap that separates the haves from the have-nots will widen. Will the developing countries honor the claims of our authors in this field, or will they encourage the growth of a black market? This is one of many problems that will arise in applying copyright to computer software.

In 1909 when the predecessor to our current Copyright Act was passed, few if any foresaw the phenomenal development of radio, television, or sound recording. Yet these three media have radically changed our culture, and for many people they have greater importance than the printed word, which was once all-powerful. Few, if any, foresaw the advent of photocopying, which now poses such a threat to the publishing industry. In each case, lawyers and their clients found themselves having to discuss new concepts in an old language. As Congress dickered and delayed, the courts were obliged to apply a sometimes-outmoded statute as best they could. The results were uneven.

Now we have caught up, but one wonders for how long. Already computer technology is creating problems, and what new technologies may arise, many of you who read this book probably know far better than I.

I am not sure there is a solution to this problem. One way or another, the copyright law has managed to adapt and survive. Some doctrines have been abandoned in the process; new ones have been acquired; others have scarcely changed in 200 years. There is a real virtue in this process, for it makes us focus on principles. Perhaps, as time goes on, we are developing a sense of what may be jettisoned in the cause of progress and what may not.

That has not been my main purpose in writing this book. My main purpose has been to acquaint you with the law as it is. However, if information really is power, what I have said may help you to contribute to the growth and orderly change of that law. That would be a benefit to all of us.

Appendix A

METHODS OF AFFIXATION AND POSITIONS OF THE COPYRIGHT NOTICE ON VARIOUS TYPES OF WORKS [37 C.F.R. CH. II §201.20]

(a) *General.* (1) This section specifies examples of methods of affixation and positions of the copyright notice on various types of works that will satisfy the notice requirement of section 401(c) of title 17 of the United States Code, as amended by Pub. L. 94–553. A notice considered "acceptable" under this regulation shall be considered to satisfy the requirement of that section that it be "affixed to the copies in such manner and location as to give reasonable notice of the claim to copyright." As provided by that section, the examples specified in this regulation shall not be considered exhaustive of methods of affixation and positions giving reasonable notice of the claim of copyright.

(2) The provisions of this section are applicable to copies publicly distributed on or after December 1, 1981. This section does not establish any rules concerning the form of the notice or the legal sufficiency of particular notices, except with respect to methods of affixation and positions of notice. The adequacy or legal sufficiency of a copyright notice is determined by

the law in effect at the time of first publication of the work.

(b) *Definitions.* For the purposes of this section:

(1) The terms "audiovisual works," "collective works," "copies," "device," "fixed," "machine," "motion picture," "pictorial, graphic, and sculptural works," and their variant forms, have the meanings given to them in section 101 of title 17.

(2) "Title 17" means title 17 of the United States Code, as amended by Pub. L. 94–553.

(3) In the case of a work consisting preponderantly of leaves on which the work is printed or otherwise reproduced on both sides, a "page" is one side of a leaf; where the preponderance of the leaves are printed on one side only, the terms "page" and "leaf" mean the same.

(4) A work is published in "book form" if the copies embodying it consist of multiple leaves bound, fastened, or assembled in predetermined order, as, for example, a volume, booklet, pamphlet, or multipage folder. For the purpose of this section, a work need not consist of textual matter in order to be considered published in "book form."

(5) A "title page" is a page, or two consecutive pages facing each other, appearing at or near the front of the copies of work published in book form, on which the complete title of the work is prominently stated and on which the names of the author or authors, the name of the publisher, the place of publication, or some combination of them, are given.

(6) The meaning of the terms "front," "back," "first," "last," and "following," when used in connection with works published in book form, will vary in relation to the physical form of the copies, depending upon the particular language in which the work is written.

(7) In the case of a work published in book form with a hard or soft cover, the "front page" and "back page" of the copies are the outsides of the front and back covers; where there is no cover, the "front page," and "back page" are the pages visible at the front and back of the copies before they are opened.

(8) A "masthead" is a body of information appearing in approximately the same location in most issues of a newspaper, magazine, journal, review, or other periodical or serial, typically containing the title of the periodical or serial, information about the staff, periodicity of issues, operation, and subscription and editorial policies, of the publication.

(9) A "single-leaf work" is a work published in copies consisting of a single leaf, including copies on which the work is printed or otherwise reproduced on either one side or on both sides of the leaf, and also folders which, without cutting or tearing the copies, can be opened out to form a single leaf. For the purpose of this section, a work need not consist of textual matter in order to be considered a "single-leaf work."

(c) *Manner of Affixation and Position Generally.* (1) In all cases dealt with in this section, the acceptability of a notice depends upon its being permanently legible to an ordinary user of the work under normal conditions of use, and affixed to the copies in such manner and position that, when affixed, it is not concealed from view upon reasonable examination.

(2) Where, in a particular case, a notice does not appear in one of the precise locations prescribed in this section but a person looking in one of those locations would be reasonably certain to find a notice in another somewhat different location, that notice will be acceptable under this section.

(d) *Works Published in Book Form.* In the case of works published in book form, a notice reproduced on the copies in any of the following positions is acceptable:

(1) The title page, if any;

(2) The page immediately following the title page, if any;

(3) Either side of the front cover, if any; or, if there is no front cover, either side of the front leaf of the copies;

(4) Either side of the back cover, if any; or, if there is no back cover, either side of the back leaf of the copies;

(5) The first page of the main body of the work;

(6) The last page of the main body of the work;

(7) Any page between the front page and the first page of the main body of the work, if: (i) There are no more than ten pages between the front page and the first page of the main body of the work; and (ii) the notice is reproduced prominently and is set apart from other matter on the page where it appears;

(8) Any page between the last page of the main body of the work and back page, if : (i) There are no more than ten pages between the last page of the main body of the work and the back page; and (ii) the notice is reproduced prominently and is set apart from the other matter on the page where it appears.

(9) In the case of a work published as an issue of a periodical or serial, in addition to any of the locations listed in paragraphs (d)(1) through (8) of this section, a notice is acceptable if it is located: (i) As a part of, or adjacent to, the masthead; (ii) on the page containing the masthead if the notice is reproduced prominently and is set apart from the other matter appearing on the page; or (iii) adjacent to a prominent heading, appearing at or near the front of the issue, containing the title of the periodical or serial and any combination of the volume and issue number and date of the issue.

(10) In the case of musical work, in addition to any of the locations listed in paragraphs (d)(l) through (9)

of this section, a notice is acceptable if it is located on the first page of music.

(e) *Single-Leaf Works.* In the case of single-leaf works, a notice reproduced on the copies anywhere on the front or back of the leaf is acceptable.

(f) *Contributions to Collective Works.* For a separate contribution to a collective work to be considered to "bear its own notice of copyright," as provided by 17 U.S.C. 404, a notice reproduced on the copies in any of the following positions is acceptable:

(1) Where the separate contribution is reproduced on a single page, a notice is acceptable if it appears: (i) Under the title of the contribution on that page; (ii) adjacent to the contribution; or (iii) on the same page if, through format, wording, or both, the application of the notice to the particular contribution is made clear;

(2) Where the separate contribution is reproduced on more than one page of the collective work, a notice is acceptable if it appears: (i) Under a title appearing at or near the beginning of the contribution; (ii) on the first page of the main body of the contribution; (iii) immediately following the end of the contribution; or (iv) on any of the pages where the contribution appears, if: (A) The contribution is reproduced on no more than twenty pages of the collective work; (B) the notice is reproduced prominently and is set apart from other matter on the page where it appears; and (C) through format, wording, or both, the application of the notice to the particular contribution is made clear;

(3) Where the separate contribution is a musical work, in addition to any of the locations listed in paragraphs (f)(1) and (2) of this section, a notice is acceptable if it is located on the first page of music of the contribution;

(4) As an alternative to placing the notice on one of the pages where a separate contribution itself appears,

the contribution is considered to "bear its own notice" if the notice appears clearly in juxtaposition with a separate listing of the contribution by title, or if the contribution is untitled, by a description reasonably identifying the contribution: (i) on the page bearing the copyright notice for the collective work as a whole, if any; or (ii) in a clearly identified and readily-accessible table of contents or listing of acknowledgements appearing near the front or back of the collective work as a whole.

(g) *Works Reproduced in Machine-Readable Copies.* For works reproduced in machine-readable copies (such as magnetic tapes or disks, punched cards, or the like, from which the work cannot ordinarily be visually perceived except with the aid of a machine or device,[1] each of the following constitute examples of acceptable methods of affixation and position of notice:

(1) A notice embodied in the copies in machine-readable form in such a manner that on visually perceptible printouts it appears either with or near the title, or at the end of the work;

(2) A notice that is displayed at the user's terminal at sign on;

(3) A notice that is continuously on terminal display; or

(4) A legible notice reproduced durably, so as to withstand normal use, on a gummed or other label securely affixed to the copies or to a box, reel, cartridge, cassette, or other container used as a permanent receptacle for the copies.

---

1 Works published in a form requiring the use of a machine or device for purposes of optical enlargement (such as film, filmstrips, slide films, and works published in any variety of microform) and works published in visually perceptible form but used in connection with optical scanning devices, are not within this category.

(h)*Motion Pictures and Other Audiovisual Works.* (1) The following constitute examples of acceptable methods of affixation and positions of the copyright notice on motion pictures and other audiovisual works: A notice that is embodied in the copies by a photomechanical or electronic process, in such a position that it ordinarily would appear whenever the work is performed in its entirety, and that is located: (i) with or near the title; (ii) with the cast, credits, and similar information; (iii) at or immediately following the beginning of the work; or (iv) at or immediately preceding the end of the work.

(2) In the case of an untitled motion picture or other audiovisual work whose duration is sixty seconds or less, in addition to any of the locations listed in paragraph (h)(1) of this section, a notice that is embodied in the copies by a photomechanical or electronic process, in such a position that it ordinarily would appear to the projectionist or broadcaster when preparing the work for performance, is acceptable if it is located on the leader of the film or tape immediately preceding the beginning of the work.

(3) In the case of a motion picture or other audiovisual work that is distributed to the public for private use, the notice may be affixed, in addition to the locations specified in paragraph (h)(1) of this section, on the housing or container, if it is a permanent receptacle for the work.

(i) *Pictorial, Graphic, and Sculptural Works.* The following constitute examples of acceptable methods of affixation and positions of the copyright notice on various forms of pictorial, graphic, and sculptural works:

(l) Where a work is reproduced in two-dimensional copies, a notice affixed directly or by means of a label cemented, sewn, or otherwise attached durably, so as to withstand normal use, of the front or back of the copies, or to any backing, mounting, matting, framing, or other material to which the copies are durably attached, so as to withstand normal use, or in which they are permanently housed, is acceptable.

(2) Where a work is reproduced in three-dimensional copies, a notice affixed directly or by means of a label cemented, sewn, or otherwise attached durably, so as to withstand normal use, to any visible portion of the work, or to any base, mounting, framing, or other material on which the copies are durably attached, so as to withstand normal use, or in which they are permanently housed, is acceptable.

(3) Where, because of the size or physical characteristics of the material in which the work is reproduced in copies, it is impossible or extremely impracticable to affix a notice to the copies directly or by means of a durable label, a notice is acceptable if it appears on a tag that is of durable material, so as to withstand normal use, and that is attached to the copy with sufficient durability that it will remain with the copy while it is passing through its normal channels of commerce.

(4) Where a work is reproduced in copies consisting of sheet-like or strip material bearing multiple or continuous reproductions of the work, the notice may be applied: (i) To the reproduction itself; (ii) to the margin, selvage, or reverse side of the material at frequent and regular intervals; or (iii) if the material contains neither a selvage nor a reverse side, to tags and labels, attached to the copies and to any spools, reels, or containers housing them in such a way that a notice is visible while the copies are passing through their normal channels of commerce.

(5) If the work is permanently housed in a container, such as a game or puzzle box, a notice reproduced on the permanent container is acceptable.

Appendix B

FORM TX
UNITED STATES COPYRIGHT OFFICE

REGISTRATION NUMBER

	TX		TXU

EFFECTIVE DATE OF REGISTRATION

Month	Day	Year

DO NOT WRITE ABOVE THIS LINE. IF YOU NEED MORE SPACE, USE A SEPARATE CONTINUATION SHEET.

1

TITLE OF THIS WORK ▼

Touring Sunny Grenada

PREVIOUS OR ALTERNATIVE TITLES ▼

Hot Spot in the Caribbean   (alternative title)

PUBLICATION AS A CONTRIBUTION If this work was published as a contribution to a periodical, serial, or collection, give information about the collective work in which the contribution appeared.   **Title of Collective Work ▼**

U.S. Marine Journal

If published in a periodical or serial give: Volume ▼	Number ▼	Issue Date ▼	On Pages ▼
15	4	11/1/83	15-24

2

a

NAME OF AUTHOR ▼

Roberta MacFarlane

DATES OF BIRTH AND DEATH
Year Born ▼ 1941   Year Died ▼

Was this contribution to the work a "work made for hire"?
☐ Yes
☒ No

AUTHOR'S NATIONALITY OR DOMICILE
Name of Country
OR { Citizen of ▶ U.S.A.
{ Domiciled in ▶

WAS THIS AUTHOR'S CONTRIBUTION TO THE WORK
Anonymous?   ☐ Yes ☒ No
Pseudonymous?   ☐ Yes ☒ No
If the answer to either of these questions is "Yes," see detailed instructions

NATURE OF AUTHORSHIP Briefly describe nature of the material created by this author in which copyright is claimed. ▼
Text

NOTE
Under the law, the "author" of a "work made for hire" is generally the employer, not the employee (see instructions). For any part of this work that was "made for hire" check "Yes" in the space provided, give the employer (or other person for whom the work was prepared) as "Author" of that part, and leave the space for dates of birth and death blank.

b

NAME OF AUTHOR ▼

Georgina Schultz

DATES OF BIRTH AND DEATH
Year Born ▼ 1929   Year Died ▼

Was this contribution to the work a "work made for hire"?
☐ Yes
☒ No

AUTHOR'S NATIONALITY OR DOMICILE
Name of country
OR { Citizen of ▶ U.S.A.
{ Domiciled in ▶

WAS THIS AUTHOR'S CONTRIBUTION TO THE WORK
Anonymous?   ☐ Yes ☒ No
Pseudonymous?   ☐ Yes ☒ No
If the answer to either of these questions is "Yes," see detailed instructions

NATURE OF AUTHORSHIP Briefly describe nature of the material created by this author in which copyright is claimed. ▼
Photographic illustrations

c

NAME OF AUTHOR ▼

DATES OF BIRTH AND DEATH
Year Born ▼   Year Died ▼

Was this contribution to the work a "work made for hire"?
☐ Yes
☐ No

AUTHOR'S NATIONALITY OR DOMICILE
Name of country
OR { Citizen of ▶
{ Domiciled in ▶

WAS THIS AUTHOR'S CONTRIBUTION TO THE WORK
Anonymous?   ☐ Yes ☐ No
Pseudonymous?   ☐ Yes ☐ No
If the answer to either of these questions is "Yes," see detailed instructions

NATURE OF AUTHORSHIP Briefly describe nature of the material created by this author in which copyright is claimed. ▼

3

YEAR IN WHICH CREATION OF THIS WORK WAS COMPLETED This information must be given in all cases.
1983 ◀ Year

DATE AND NATION OF FIRST PUBLICATION OF THIS PARTICULAR WORK
Complete this information Month ▶ November Day ▶ 01 Year ▶ 83
ONLY if this work has been published.   U.S.A.   ◀ Nation

4

COPYRIGHT CLAIMANT(S) Name and address must be given even if the claimant is the same as the author given in space 2.▼

Carribee Publishers, Inc.
54 Manitou Drive
Conch Shell, Florida 33904

See instructions before completing this space.

APPLICATION RECEIVED

ONE DEPOSIT RECEIVED

TWO DEPOSITS RECEIVED

REMITTANCE NUMBER AND DATE

DO NOT WRITE HERE OFFICE USE ONLY

TRANSFER If the claimant(s) named here in space 4 are different from the author(s) named in space 2, give a brief statement of how the claimant(s) obtained ownership of the copyright.▼

Written transfer of all right, title, and interest.

MORE ON BACK ▶ • Complete all applicable spaces (numbers 5-11) on the reverse side of this page.
• See detailed instructions.   • Sign the form at line 10.

DO NOT WRITE HERE

Page 1 of _____ pages

EXAMINED BY

FORM TX

CHECKED BY

☐ CORRESPONDENCE
Yes

☐ DEPOSIT ACCOUNT
FUNDS USED

FOR
COPYRIGHT
OFFICE
USE
ONLY

DO NOT WRITE ABOVE THIS LINE. IF YOU NEED MORE SPACE, USE A SEPARATE CONTINUATION SHEET.

PREVIOUS REGISTRATION Has registration for this work, or for an earlier version of this work, already been made in the Copyright Office?
☒ Yes ☐ No If your answer is "Yes," why is another registration being sought? (Check appropriate box) ▼

☐ This is the first published edition of a work previously registered in unpublished form.

☐ This is the first application submitted by this author as copyright claimant.

☒ This is a changed version of the work, as shown by space 6 on this application.

If your answer is "Yes," give: **Previous Registration Number** ▼   **Year of Registration** ▼
          TX 1 – 156 – 780   1982

5

DERIVATIVE WORK OR COMPILATION Complete both space 6a & 6b for a derivative work; complete only 6b for a compilation.
a. Preexisting Material Identify any preexisting work or works that this work is based on or incorporates. ▼
    Castro's Third World Colonies (an article in U.S. Marine Journal, vol. 14, no. 1)

b. Material Added to This Work Give a brief, general statement of the material that has been added to this work and in which copyright is claimed. ▼
    Text has been substantially revised, and photographs are all new.

6

See instructions
before completing
this space.

MANUFACTURERS AND LOCATIONS If this is a published work consisting preponderantly of nondramatic literary material in English, the law may require that the copies be manufactured in the United States or Canada for full protection. If so, the names of the manufacturers who performed certain processes and the places where these processes were performed **must** be given. See instructions for details.
Names of Manufacturers ▼   **Places of Manufacture** ▼
    Typesetter: Tinker Text, Inc.   Potowatamee, Wisconsin
    Printer/Binder: Tailer Publishers   Oshkosh, Wisconsin

7

REPRODUCTION FOR USE OF BLIND OR PHYSICALLY HANDICAPPED INDIVIDUALS   A signature on this form at space 10, and a check in one of the boxes here in space 8, constitutes a non-exclusive grant of permission to the Library of Congress to reproduce and distribute solely for the blind and physically handicapped and under the conditions and limitations prescribed by the regulations of the Copyright Office: (1) copies of the work identified in space 1 of this application in Braille (or similar tactile symbols); or (2) phonorecords embodying a fixation of a reading of that work; or (3) both.
    a ☒ Copies and Phonorecords   b ☐ Copies Only   c ☐ Phonorecords Only

8

See instructions.

DEPOSIT ACCOUNT If the registration fee is to be charged to a Deposit Account established in the Copyright Office, give name and number of Account.
Name ▼   **Account Number** ▼

9

CORRESPONDENCE Give name and address to which correspondence about this application should be sent. Name/Address/Apt/City/State/Zip ▼
    Ephraim Lawless, Esq.
    Lawless & Wylde, P.C.
    200 State Street, Conch Shell, Florida   33904
                          Area Code & Telephone Number ▶

Be sure to
give your
daytime phone
◀ number.

CERTIFICATION* I, the undersigned, hereby certify that I am the
                                                    ☐ author
                          Check one ▶   ☐ other copyright claimant
                                                    ☐ owner of exclusive right(s)
of the work identified in this application and that the statements made   ☒ authorized agent of Carribee Publishers, Inc.
by me in this application are correct to the best of my knowledge.   Name of author or other copyright claimant, or owner of exclusive right(s) ▲

10

Typed or printed name and date ▼ If this is a published work, this date must be the same as or later than the date of publication given in space 3.
    Manuel Hidalgo, President   date ▶

☞ Handwritten signature (X) ▼

**MAIL
CERTIFI-
CATE TO**

Name ▼
    Ephraim Lawless, Esq.

Number/Street/Apartment Number ▼
    Lawless & Wylde, P.C.
    200 State Street

**Certificate
will be
mailed in
window
envelope**

City/State/ZIP ▼
    Conch Shell, Florida   33904

Have you:
• Completed all necessary spaces?
• Signed your application in space 10?
• Enclosed check or money order for $10 payable to *Register of Copyrights*?
• Enclosed your deposit material with the application and fee?

MAIL TO: Register of Copyrights, Library of Congress, Washington, D.C. 20559.

11

* 17 U.S.C. § 506(e): Any person who knowingly makes a false representation of a material fact in the application for copyright registration provided for by section 409, or in any written statement filed in connection with the application, shall be fined not more than $2,500.

★ U.S. GOVERNMENT PRINTING OFFICE: 1983: 381-278/503

August 1983—300,000

Appendix C

"Best Edition" of Published Copyrighted Works for the Collections of the Library of Congress*

The Copyright Law (Title 17, United States Code) requires that copies or phonorecords deposited in the Copyright Office be of the "best edition" of the work. The law states that "The 'best edition' of a work is the edition, published in the United States at any time before the date of deposit, that the Library of Congress determines to be most suitable for its purposes."

When two or more editions of the same version of a work have been published, the one of the highest quality is generally considered to be the best edition. In judging quality, the Library of Congress will adhere to the criteria set forth below in all but exceptional circumstances.

Where differences between editions represent variations in copyrightable content, each edition is a separate version and "best edition" standards based on such differences do not apply. Each such version is a separate work for the purposes of the Copyright Law.

Appearing below are lists of criteria to be applied in determining the best edition of each of several types of material. The criteria are listed in descending order of importance. In deciding between two editions, a criterion-by-criterion comparison should be made. The edition which first fails to satisfy a criterion is to be considered of inferior quality and will not be an acceptable deposit. For example, if a comparison is made between two hardbound editions of a book, one a trade edition printed on acid-free paper and the other a specially bound edition printed on average paper, the former will be the best edition because the type of paper is a more important criterion than the binding.

Under regulations of the Copyright Office, potential depositors may request authorization to deposit copies or phonorecords of other than the best edition of a specific work (e.g., a microform rather than a printed edition of a serial).

I. PRINTED TEXTUAL MATTER

A. *Paper, Binding, and Packaging:*

1. Archival-quality rather than less-permanent paper.

2. Hard cover rather than soft cover.

3. Library binding rather than commercial binding.

4. Trade edition rather than book club edition.

5. Sewn rather than glue-only binding.

6. Sewn or glued rather than stapled or spiral-bound.

7. Stapled rather than spiral-bound or plastic-bound.

8. Bound rather than looseleaf, except when future looseleaf insertions are to be issued.

9. Slipcased rather than nonslipcased.

10. With protective folders rather than without (for broadsides).

11. Rolled rather than folded (for broadsides).

12. With protective coatings rather than without (except broadsides, which should not be coated).

B. *Rarity:*
1. Special limited edition having the greatest number of special features.
2. Other limited edition rather than trade edition.
3. Special binding rather than trade binding.

C. *Illustrations:*
1. Illustrated rather than unillustrated.
2. Illustrations in color rather than black and white.

D. *Special Features:*
1. With thumb notches or index tabs rather than without.
2. With aids to use such as overlays and magnifiers rather than without.

E. *Size:*
1. Larger rather than smaller sizes. (Except that large-type editions for the partially-sighted are not required in place of editions employing type of more conventional size.)

II. PHOTOGRAPHS

A. Size and finish, in descending order of preference:
1. The most widely distributed edition.
2. 8 × 10-inch glossy print.
3. Other size or finish.

B. Unmounted rather than mounted.

C. Archival-quality rather than less-permanent paper stock or printing process.

III. MOTION PICTURES

A. Film rather than another medium. Film editions are listed below in descending order of preference.
1. Preprint material, by special arrangement.
2. Film gauge in which most widely distributed.
3. 35 mm rather than 16 mm.
4. 16 mm rather than 8 mm.
5. Special formats (e.g., 65 mm) only in exceptional cases.
6. Open reel rather than cartridge or cassette.

*This excerpt is taken from Volume 43, No. 2 of the *Federal Register* for Wednesday, January 4, 1978 (p. 766).

B. Videotape rather than videodisc. Videotape editions are listed below in descending order of preference.
1. Tape gauge in which most widely distributed.
2. Two-inch tape.
3. One-inch tape.
4. Three-quarter-inch tape cassette.
5. One-half-inch tape cassette.

IV. OTHER GRAPHIC MATTER

A. *Paper and Printing:*
1. Archival quality rather than less-permanent paper.
2. Color rather than black and white.

B. *Size and Content:*
1. Larger rather than smaller size.
2. In the case of cartographic works, editions with the greatest amount of information rather than those with less detail.

C. *Rarity:*
1. The most widely distributed edition rather than one of limited distribution.
2. In the case of a work published only in a limited, numbered edition, one copy outside the numbered series but otherwise identical.
3. A photographic reproduction of the original, by special arrangement only.

D. *Text and Other Materials:*
1. Works with annotations, accompanying tabular or textual matter, or other interpretative aids rather than those without them.

E. *Binding and Packaging:*
1. Bound rather than unbound.
2. If editions have different binding, apply the criteria in I.A.2–I.A.7, above.
4. Rolled rather than folded.
5. With protective coatings rather than without.

V. PHONORECORDS

A. Disc rather than tape.

B. With special enclosures rather than without.

C. Open-reel rather than cartridge.

D. Cartridge rather than cassette.

E. Quadraphonic rather than stereophonic.

F. True stereophonic rather than monaural.

G. Monaural rather than electronically rechanneled stereo.

VI. MUSICAL COMPOSITIONS

A. *Fullness of Score:*
1. *Vocal music:*
a. With orchestral accompaniment—
i. Full score and parts, if any, rather than conductor's score and parts, if any. (In cases of compositions published only by rental, lease, or lending, this requirement is reduced to full score only.)
ii. Conductor's score and parts, if any, rather than condensed score and parts, if any. (In cases of compo-

sitions published only by rental, lease, or lending, this requirement is reduced to conductor's score only.)
b. Unaccompanied: Open score (each part on separate staff) rather than closed score (all parts condensed to two staves).
2. *Instrumental music:*
a. Full score and parts, if any, rather than conductor's score and parts, if any. (In cases of compositions published only by rental, lease, or lending, this requirement is reduced to full score only.)
b. Conductor's score and parts, if any, rather than condensed score and parts, if any. (In cases of compositions published only by rental, lease, or lending, this requirement is reduced to conductor's score only.)

B. *Printing and Paper:*
1. Archival-quality rather than less-permanent paper.

C. *Binding and Packaging:*
1. Special limited editions rather than trade editions.
2. Bound rather than unbound.
3. If editions have different binding, apply the criteria in I.A.2–I.A.12, above.
4. With protective folders rather than without.

VII. MICROFORMS

A. *Related Materials:*
1. With indexes, study guides, or other printed matter rather than without.

B. *Permanence and Appearance:*
1. Silver halide rather than any other emulsion.
2. Positive rather than negative.
3. Color rather than black and white.

C. *Format (newspapers and newspaper-formatted serials):*
1. Reel microfilm rather than any other microform.

D. *Format (all other materials):*
1. Microfiche rather than reel microfilm.
2. Reel microfilm rather than microform cassettes.
3. Microfilm cassettes rather than micro-opaque prints.

E. *Size:*
1. 35 mm rather than 16 mm.

VIII. WORKS EXISTING IN MORE THAN ONE MEDIUM

Editions are listed below in descending order of preference.

A. Newspapers, dissertations and theses, newspaper-formatted serials:
1. Microform.
2. Printed matter.

B. All other materials:
1. Printed matter.
2. Microform.
3. Phonorecord.
(Effective: January 1, 1978.)

For further information on Copyright Office deposit regulations, see Part 202 of 37 CFR, Chapter II, or write to the Register of Copyrights, Library of Congress, Washington, D.C. 20559.

Appendix D

REGISTRATION OF COMPUTER PROGRAMS
AND DATA BASES

If you are considering registering copyright in (a) an unpublished program or data base that is fixed only in object form (what the regulations call "machine-readable form"), or (b) a published program or data base that is published only in object form, the regulations call for the deposit of the following identifying material instead of a copy of the object code:

1. In the case of a program, the first twenty-five pages or similar units, and the last twenty-five pages or similar units, in visually perceptible form, along with, if the work is published, the page or other unit containing the copyright notice. "Visually perceptible form" means: on paper or in microform.

2. For a data base on any single subject, the first and last twenty-five pages or similar units in visually perceptible form.

3. For a data base made up of data files covering two or more separate and distinct subjects, either fifty complete data records from each file, or the entire file, whichever is less, in visually perceptible form. If you choose the former route, you must include a descriptive statement, typed or printed, containing this information:

• the title of the data base;

• the name and address of the copyright claimant;

• the name and content of each separate file, including subject matter, origins of the data, and the approximate number of records in the file;

• if the work is published, an exact description of the copyright notice that is put on the work and the manner or frequency with which it is displayed—e.g., at user's terminal only at sign on, or on printouts, or whatever.

4. For either sort of data base, if you affix a visually perceptible notice to the work or to the container in which you publish it, you must include a sample of that notice with your deposit.

All these rules apply only to registration deposit; the Library of Congress does not require deposit of these works.

It should be noted that the Copyright Office is accepting copies of object code as deposit copies under what it calls the "rule of doubt." This means that the Copyright Office, in granting registration, is expressing no opinion on whether the object code actually embodies the work being registered. The registration is thus more open to attack than one for which identifying material has been deposited.

Appendix E

WARNINGS OF COPYRIGHT FOR USE BY CERTAIN LIBRARIES AND ARCHIVES [37 C.F.R. CH. II §201.14]

(a) *Definitions.* (1) A "Display Warning of Copyright" is a notice under paragraphs (d) (2) and (e) (2) of section 108 of Title 17 of the United States Code as amended by Pub. L. 94-553. As required by those sections the "Display Warning of Copyright" is to be displayed at the place where orders for copies or phono-records are accepted by certain libraries and archives.

(2) An "Order Warning of Copyright" is a notice under paragraphs (d) (2) and (e) (2) of section 108 of Title 17 of the United States Code as amended by Pub. L. 94-553. As required by those sections the "Order Warning of Copyright" is to be included on printed forms supplied by certain libraries and archives and used by their patrons for ordering copies or phonorecords.

(b) *Contents.* A Display Warning of Copyright and an Order Warning of Copyright shall consist of a verbatim reproduction of the following notice, printed in such size and form and displayed in such manner as to comply with paragraph (c) of this section:

NOTICE
WARNING CONCERNING COPYRIGHT RESTRICTIONS

The copyright law of the United States (Title 17, United States Code) governs the making of photocopies or other reproductions of copyrighted material.

Under certain conditions specified in the law, libraries and archives are authorized to furnish a photocopy or other reproduction. One of these specified conditions is that the photocopy or reproduction is not to be "used for any purpose other than private study, scholarship, or research." If a user makes a request for, or later uses, a photocopy or a reproduction for purposes in excess of "fair use," that user may be liable for copyright infringement.

This institution reserves the right to refuse to accept a copying order if, in its judgment, fulfillment of the order would involve violation of copyright law.

(c) *Form and Manner of Use.* (1) A Display Warning of Copyright shall be printed on heavy paper or other durable material in type at least 18 points in size, and shall be displayed prominently, in such manner and location as to be clearly visible, legible, and comprehensible to a casual observer within the immediate vicinity of the place where orders are accepted.

(2) An Order Warning of Copyright shall be printed within a box located prominently on the order form itself, either on the front side of the form or immediately adjacent to the space calling for the name or signature of the person using the form. The notice shall be printed in type size no smaller than that used predominantly throughout the form, and in no case shall the type size be smaller than 8 points. The notice shall be printed in such manner as to be clearly legible, comprehensible, and readily apparent to a casual reader of the form.

Notes

Chapter 1

1. 17 U.S.C. §102(a).

2. 17 U.S.C. §301.

3. *See, e.g.,* Hoehling v. Universal City Studios, Inc., 618 F.2d 972 (2d Cir. 1980), *cert. denied* 449 U.S. 841 (1980); Miller v. Universal City Studios, Inc., 650 F.2d 1365 (5th Cir. 1981).

4. Sheldon v. Metro-Goldwyn Pictures Corp., 81 F.2d 49, 54 (2d Cir. 1936).

5. 17 U.S.C. §101.

6. Alfred Bell & Co. v. Catalda Fine Arts, Inc., 191 F.2d 99 (2d Cir. 1951), *aff'g* 74 F. Supp. 973 (S.D.N.Y. 1947); Alva Studios, Inc. v. Winninger, 177 F. Supp. 265 (S.D.N.Y. 1959).

7. 17 U.S.C. § 103(b).

8. L. Batlin & Son, Inc. v. Snyder, 536 F.2d 436 (2d Cir. 1976); Durham Industries, Inc. v. Tomy Corp., 630 F.2d 905 (2d Cir. 1980); Gracen v. Bradford Exchange, 698 F.2d 300 (7th Cir. 1983); Sunset House Distrib. Corp. v. Doran, 304 F.2d 251 (9th Cir. 1962), *aff'g* 197 F. Supp. 940 (S.D.Cal. 1961). *See also* Knickerbocker Toy Co., Inc. v. Winterbrook Toy Corp., 216 U.S.P.Q. 621 (D.N.H. 1982).

9. A lucid and interesting discussion of this problem may be found in Oppenheimer, "Originality in Art Reproductions: 'Variations' in Search of a Theme," *Bull. Copr. Society* vol. 26, no. 1, 1978.

10 *See, e.g.,* Official Aviation Guide Co. v. American Aviation Associates, 150 F.2d 173 (7th Cir. 1945); Leon v. Pacific Tel. & Tel. Co., 91 F. 2d 484 (9th Cir. 1937); R.R. Donnelley & Sons Co. v. Haber, 43 F. Supp. 456 (E.D.N.Y. 1942); Jeweler's Circular Pub. Co. v. Keystone Publ. Co., 281 Fed. 83 (2d Cir. 1922).

11. Sometimes these rules are taken too far, as in Leon v. Pacific Tel. & Tel. Co., *supra*; *see* Triangle Publications, Inc. v. Sports Eye, Inc., 415 F. Supp. 682 (E.D.Pa. 1976). *Compare* National Business Lists, Inc. v. Dun & Bradstreet, Inc., 215 U.S.P.Q. 595 (N.D.Ill. 1982) with New York Times Co. v. Roxbury Data Interface, Inc., 434 F.Supp. 217 (S.D.N.Y. 1977).

12. Gilliam v. American Broadcasting Companies, Inc., 538 F.2d 14 (2d Cir. 1976).

13. 101 U.S. 99 (1880).

14. Harcourt, Brace & World Inc. v. Graphic Controls Corp., 329 F.Supp. 517 (S.D.N.Y. 1971); Manpower, Inc. v. Temporary Help of Harrisburg, Inc., 246 F.Supp. 788 (E.D.Pa. 1965).

15. Morrissey v. Procter & Gamble Co., 379 F.2d 675 (1st Cir. 1967).

16. 17 U.S.C. §102(a).

17. Leon v. Pacific Tel. & Tel., *supra*; Amsterdam v. Triangle Publications, Inc., 189 F.2d 104 (3rd Cir. 1951).

18. *See, e.g.,* Metropolitan Opera Association, Inc. v. Wagner-Nichols Recorder Corp., 199 Misc. 786, 101 N.Y.S.2d 483 (1950), *aff'd,* 279 App. Div. 632, 107 N.Y.S.2d 795 (1951).

19. *See, e.g.,* Lennon v. Pulsebeat News, Inc., 143 U.S.P.Q. 309 (N.Y.Sup.Ct. 1964); Sinatra v. Goodyear

Tire & Rubber Co., 435 F.2d 711 (9th Cir. 1979); Booth v. Colgate-Palmolive Co., 362 F.Supp. 343 (S.D.N.Y. 1973).

20. *See, e.g.,* Becker v. Loew's, Inc., 133 F.2d 889 (7th Cir. 1943).

21. Paramore v. Mack Sennett, 9 F.2d 66 (S.D.Cal. 1925); *cf.* Duff v. Kansas City Star Co., 229 F.2d 320 (8th Cir. 1962). The scope of the law on unfair competition has been severely limited in recent years. Federal copyright law now preempts state laws in the field, to the extent they purport to protect rights equivalent to rights under copyright in works fixed in tangible form, whether or not they are copyrightable. 17 U.S.C. §301; H.R. Rep. No. 94–1476, 94th Cong., 2d Ses. 130–133 (1976). (This, the House of Representatives Report for the Copyright Act of 1976, will be referred to hereafter as "H. Rep.") This does not apply quite so broadly to causes of action arising before 1978. There is no reason to feel it would restrict protection of titles, since titles are regarded as trademarks under federal law, not as works of authorship.

22. H. Rep., pp. 53–54.

23. H. Rep., p. 55.

24. *Ibid.*; 17 U.S.C. §§101, 113(b); H. Rep., p. 105.

25. *Ibid.; see also, e.g.,* Muller v. Triborough Bridge Authority, 43 F. Supp. 298 (S.D.N.Y. 1974); DeSilva Construction Corp. v. Herrald, 213 F.Supp. 184 (N.D.Fla. 1962); Imperial Homes Corp. v. Lamont, 458 F.2. 895 (5th Cir. 1972); *but see* Herman Frankel Organization v. Wolfe, 184 U.S.P.Q. 819 (E.D.Mich. 1974). *Cf.* 17 U.S.C. §106(2), and, *e.g.* King Features Syndicate v. Fleischer, 299 Fed. 533 (2d Cir. 1924).

26. H. Rep., p. 55.

27. *Ibid.*

28. *See, e.g.,* Nichols v. Universal Pictures Corp., 45 F.2d 119 (1930), *cert. denied* 282 U.S. 902 (1931).

29. Warner Bros. Pictures, Inc. v. Columbia Broadcasting System, Inc., 216 F.2d 945 (9th Cir. 1954); *see* Borroughs v. Metro-Goldwyn-Mayer, Inc., 683 F.2d 610 (2d Cir. 1982).

30. Williams Electronics, Inc. v. Artic International, Inc., 685 F.2d 870 (3rd Cir. 1982); Apple Computer, Inc. v. Franklin Computer Corp., CCH Copr.L.Dec. ¶25,565 (3rd Cir. 1983), *cert. denied* _____ U.S. _____ (1984); Apple Computer, Inc. v. Formula International Inc., 562 F.Supp. 775 (N.D.Cal. 1983).

31. Final Report of the National Commission on New Technological Use of Copyrighted Works, pp. 9–38. Prior law had held that if a work was not intelligible, even with magnification, to the human eye, it neither infringed copyright nor was entitled to copyright. White-Smith Music Publishing Co. v. Apollo Co., 209 U.S. 1 (1908); Corcoran v. Montgomery Ward & Co., Inc., 121 F.2d 572 (9th Cir. 1941). At first, it was thought that this doctrine might apply to object code, Data Cash Systems, Inc. v. JS&A Group, Inc., 480 F.Supp. 1063 (N.D.Ill. 1979), *aff'd on other grounds*, 628 F.2d 1038 (7th Cir. 1980). *See* Stern, Another Look at Copyright Protection of Software: Did the 1980 Act Do Anything for Object Code?, Computer Law Journal Vol.III, No.1 (Fall, 1981), pp. 1–17.

32. Paine, Webber, Jackson & Curtis, Inc. v. Merrill, Lynch, Pierce, Fenner & Smith, Inc., 26 P.T.C.J. 143 (D.Del. 1983).

33. 17 U.S.C. §102(b).

34. Diamond v. Diehr, 450 U.S. 175 (1981); *see also* Diamond v. Bradley, 600 F.2d 807 (C.C.P.A. 1979), *aff'd by an equally divided court*, 450 U.S. 381 (1981).

35. Final Report of CONTU, *supra*, at pp. 19–21.

36. Chamberlin v. Uris Sales Corp., 150 F.2d 512 (2d Cir. 1945); *see* Brief English Systems v. Owen, 48 F.2d 555 (2d Cir. 1931) and Universal Athletic Sales Co. v. Salkeld, 511 F.2d 904 (3rd Cir. 1975); *cf.* the factually

ambiguous case of Runge v. Lee, 441 F.2d 479 (9th Cir. 1971) and Justice Douglas's dissent to the denial of certiorari thereon, 404 U.S. 887 (1971).

37. Williams Electronics, Inc. v. Artic International, Inc., *supra*.

Chapter 2   1. 17 U.S.C. §101.

2. Shapiro, Bernstein & Co. v. Jerry Vogel Music Co., Inc., 161 F.2d 406, 410 (2d Cir., 1946, 1947), *cert. denied* 331 U.S. 820 (1942).

3. H. Rep., p. 120.

4. Sweet Music, Inc. v. Melrose Music Corp., 189 F.Supp. 655, 659 (S.D.Cal. 1960).

5. Melville B. Nimmer, Nimmer on Copyright (N.Y., Matthew Bender, 1980), §6.10[C].

6. Donaldson Publishing Co. v. Bregman, Vocco & Conn, Inc., 375 F.2d 639 (2d Cir. 1967); Town of Clarkson v. Reeder, 26 P.T.C.J. 184 (S.D.N.Y. 1983).

7. Williams v. Weisser, 78 Cal. Rptr. 542 (1969).

8. 17 U.S.C. §201(b).

9. Van Cleef & Arpels, Inc. v. Schechter, 308 F. Supp. 674 (S.D.N.Y. 1969); Scherr v. Universal Match Corp., 417 F.2d 497 (2nd Cir. 1969).

10. 17. U.S.C. §101.

11. *See* Ringer and Flacks, "Applicability of the Universal Copyright Convention to Certain Works in the Public Domain in their Country of Origin," *Bull. Copr. Society* vol. 27, no. 3 (1980).

12. *See, e.g.*, Public Affairs Associates, Inc. v. Rickover, 268 F. Supp. 444 (D.D.C. 1967); Bell v. Combined Registry Co., 536 F.2d 164 (7th Cir. 1976).

13. *See* Avedon v. Exstein, 141 F. Supp. 278 (S.D.N.Y. 1956).

14. 17 U.S.C. §201(b).

15. 17 U.S.C. §109(b).

16. Avedon v. Exstein, *supra*.

17. This is particularly troublesome in light of the preemption question. 17 U.S.C. §301(a).

18. The Final Report of CONTU, *supra*, only brushes against this problem, at p. 45 *et seq*. Its discussion of the general area seems sketchy.

19. 17 U.S.C. §201(d)(2).

20. 17 U.S.C. §202.

21. 17 U.S.C. §109(b).

22. 17 U.S.C. §302(b).

23. 17 U.S.C. §302(c).

Chapter 3   1. 17 U.S.C. §201(e).

2. David Grossman Designs, Inc. v. Bortin, 347 F. Supp. 1150 (N.D. Ill. 1972); Gerlach-Barklow Co. v. Morris S. Bendien, 23 F.2d 159 (2nd Cir. 1927).

3. 17 U.S.C. §204(a).

4. *See, e.g.,* with regard to time limitations, 17 U.S.C. §203(b)(6); Viacom Int'l, Inc. v. Tandem Productions, Inc., 368 F. Supp. 1264 (S.D.N.Y. 1974), *aff'd* 526 F.2d 593 (2nd Cir. 1975).

5. *See, e.g.,* Bartsch v. Metro-Goldwyn Mayer, Inc., 391 F. 2d 150 (2nd Cir. 1968); Ettore v. Philco Television Broadcasting Corp., 229 F.2d 481 (3rd Cir. 1956). Prof. Nimmer lists many more of these cases at §10.10[B] of Nimmer, *op. cit.*

6. 17 U.S.C. §201(c).

7. Mills Music v. Cromwell Music, 126 F. Supp. 54 (S.D.N.Y. 1954); *cf.* Viacom Int'l, Inc. v. Tandem Productions, Inc., *supra*.

8. 17 U.S.C. §204(a).

9. 17 U.S.C. §204(a). Eden Toys v. Florelee, 697 F.2d 27 (2d Cir. 1982).

10. 17 U.S.C. §204(b).

11. 17 U.S.C. §405(a)(3).

12. 17 U.S.C. §708(a)(4).

13. 17 U.S.C. §§205(b), 708(a)(9).

14. 17 U.S.C. §205(c).

15. 17 U.S.C. §205(e).

16. *Ibid.*

17. 17 U.S.C. §205(f).

18. 17 U.S.C. §205(d). The copyright owner does not have to record documents showing his entire chain of title, only the immediate document by which he obtained title. Swarowski America, Ltd. v. Silver Deer, Ltd., 537 F. Supp. 1201 (D.Colo. 1982).

19. 17 U.S.C. §101.

17. U.S.C. §203(a) (5).

21. 17 U.S.C. §§203(a), 203(b) (5).

22. *Ibid.*

23. 17 U.S.C. §203(b)(1); Harry Fox Agency, Inc. v. Mills Music, Inc. CCH Copr. L. Dec. ¶25,589 (2d Cir. 1983).

24. 17 U.S.C. §§101, 203(a).

25. 17 U.S.C. §203(a)(3).

26. *See generally* 17 U.S.C. §203.

27. 17 U.S.C. §203(b).

28. 17 U.S.C. §203(b)(4).

29. 17 U.S.C. §203(b)(3).

30. *Ibid.*

Chapter 4   1. 17 U.S.C. §101; Jewelers' Mercantile Agency, Ltd. v. Jewelers' Weekly Pub. Co., 155 N.Y. 241, 49 N.E. 872 (1897).

2. Gottsberger v. Aldine Book Pub. Co., 33 Fed. 381 (C.C.D. Mass. 1887); Bobbs-Merrill Co. v. Straus, 147 Fed. 15 (2nd Cir. 1906), *aff'd* 210 U.S. 339 (1908).

3. 17 U.S.C. §101.

4. Grandma Moses Properties, Inc. v. This Week Magazine, 117 F. Supp. 348 (S.D.N.Y. 1953); *cf.* remarks of Rep. Kastenmeier, 122 Cong. Rec. No. 10, 874–5 (daily ed. Sept. 22, 1976).

5. 17 U.S.C. §101.

6. 17 U.S.C. §101; White v. Kimmell, 193 F.2d 744 (9th Cir. 1952).

7. Marvin Worth Prods. v. Superior Films Corp., 319 F. Supp. 1269 (S.D.N.Y 1970); *see generally* Nimmer, *op. cit.*; §4.10.

8. Folsom v. Marsh, 9 Fed. Cas. 342, No. 4901 (C.C. Mass. 1841).

9. 17 U.S.C. §101.

10. 17 U.S.C. §404(a). This does not apply to ads inserted on behalf of the copyright owner of the collective work.

11. 17 U.S.C. §402.

12. 17 U.S.C. §401(b)(2).

13. 17 U.S.C. §§401(b)(3);408(a).

14. 17 U.S.C. §402(c).

15. 17 U.S.C. §506(c).

16. 17 U.S.C. §406(a).

17. 17 U.S.C. §406(b).

18. 17 U.S.C. §405; H. Rep. pp. 145–6.

19. Russell v. Price, 448 F. Supp. 303 (C.D. Cal. 1977).

20. In recent cases, it has been held that omission from 1% of 40,000 copies was permissible, whereas omission from 22–37% of 1335 copies was not. Original Appalachian Artworks, Inc. v. The Toy Loft, Inc., 684 F.2d 821 (11th Cir. 1982); King v. Burnett, CCH Copr.L.Dec. ¶25,489 (D.D.C. 1982).

21. 17 U.S.C. §103(b); Grove Press, Inc. v. Greenleaf Publishing Co., 247 F.Supp. 518 (S.D.N.Y. 1965); Russell v. Price, 612 F.2d 1123 (9th Cir. 1979), *cert. denied* 446 U.S. 952 (1980).

22. 17 U.S.C. §405(b).

23. Technicon Medical Information Systems Corp. v. Green Bay Packaging Inc., 687 F.2d 1032 (7th Cir. 1982), *cert. denied* 103 S.Ct. 732 (1983); *see also* M.Bryce & Associates, Inc. v. Gladstone, 215 U.S.P.Q. 81 (Wisc. Ct. of App., 1982).

24. As the legislative history notes, "a work is 'published' if one or more copies or phonorecords embodying it are distributed to the public—that is, generally to persons under no explicit or implicit restrictions with respect to disclosure of its contents. . . ." H.Rep., p.138.

Chapter 5   1. 17 U.S.C. §411(a).

2. 17 U.S.C. §412. The special exemption for films first fixed at time of broadcast is only available if advance notice is given to an infringer. 17 U.S.C. §411(b), 45 F.R. 50823.

3. 17 U.S.C. §409.

4. 17 U.S.C. §601 *et seq.*

5. 17 U.S.C. §506(e).

6. 17 U.S.C. §708(a).

7. 17 U.S.C. §407.

8. 37 C.F.R. Ch. II §202.19(f).

9. 17 U.S.C. §407(d).

10. 37 C.F.R. Ch.II §202.19.

11. 37 C.F.R. Ch.II §202.20.

12. 37 C.F.R. Ch.II §202.21.

13. 17 U.S.C. §408(c)(2).

14. 17 U.S.C. §710; 37 C.F.R. Ch.II §201.15.

Chapter 6   1. 17 U.S.C. §117.

2. 17 U.S.C. §114(a). Congress is considering changing this rule.

3. 17 U.S.C. §110.

4. 17 U.S.C. §111(a),(b).

5. 17 U.S.C. §112(b).

6. 37 C.F.R. Ch.II §201.13.

7. 17 U.S.C. §112(d).

8. 17 U.S.C. §110(5).

9. 17 U.S.C. §110(3).

10. 17 U.S.C. §113(c).

11. N.Y. General Business Law, Art. 12-J, §228-m-q; Calif. Civil Code §987.

12. Calif. Civil Code §986.

Chapter 7   1. 17 U.S.C. §115. For the royalty rates, see 46 Fed. Reg. 55277 (Dec.23,1981), and Recording Industry Assoc. v. Copyright Royalty Tribunal, 662 F.2d 1 (D.C.Cir. 1981).

2. 37 C.F.R. Ch.II §201.18.

3. *Ibid.*

4. Sec. 1(e) of the 1909 Act (i.e., of Title 17 as amended prior to enactment of the Copyright Act of 1976); 17 U.S.C. §116(a).

5. 17 U.S.C. §116(b).

6. Fortnightly Corp. v. United Artists Television, Inc., 392 U.S. 390 (1968).

7. 17 U.S.C. §112. The royalty rates are found at 37 C.F.R. Ch.III Part 308.

8. 17 U.S.C. §501(b),(c),(d).

9. 17 U.S.C. §118.

10. 37 C.F.R. Ch.III Part 304, as amended most recently by 47 F.R. 57923 (Dec. 29, 1982).

Chapter 8   1. A stimulating discussion of this is Prof. Benjamin Kaplan's book, *An Unhurried View of Copyright* (New York: Columbia Univ. Press, 1967).

2. Judge Learned Hand, writing in Nichols v. Universal Pictures Corp., 45 F.2d 119 (2nd Cir. 1930), *cert. den.* 282 U.S. 902 (1931).

3. *See, e.g.,* Harold Lloyd Corp. v. Witwer, 65 F.2d 1 (9th Cir. 1933); Twentieth Century Fox-Film Corp. v. Stonesifer, 140 F.2d 579 (9th Cir. 1944).

4. Sheldon v. Metro-Goldwyn Pictures Corp., 81 F.2d 49 (2nd Cir., 1936).

5. Bleistein v. Donaldson Lithographing Co., 188 U.S. 239 (1903).

6. Burrow-Giles Lithographic Co. v. Sarony, 111 U.S. 53 (1884).

7. 17 U.S.C. §301(b)(2).

8. 17 U.S.C. §501(b).

9. *Ibid.*

10. 17 U.S.C. §504(b).

11. 17 U.S.C. §504(c).

12. 17 U.S.C. §505.

13. 17 U.S.C. §506(a).

14. 17 U.S.C. §107. On the first criterion, see Rubin v. Boston Magazine Co., 645 F.2d 80 (1st Cir. 1981). On the fourth, see New Boston Television, Inc. v. Entertainment Sports Programming Network, Inc., 215 U.S.P.Q. 755 (D. Mass. 1981); DC Comics, Inc. v. Reel Fantasy, Inc., 696 F.2d 24 (2d Cir. 1982).

15. Publications Int'l Ltd. v. Bally Mfg. Corp., 215 U.S.P.Q. 861 (N.D.Ill. 1982).

16. *See* Meredith Corp. v. Harper & Row, Publishers, Inc., 378 F. Supp. 686 (S.D.N.Y. 1977), *affd.* 500 F.2d 1221 (2nd Cir. 1974).

17. 17 U.S.C. §113(c); Italian Book Corp. v. American Broadcasting Companies, Inc., 458 F. Supp. 65 (S.D.N.Y. 1978).

18. 131 F. Supp. 165 (S.D. Cal. 1955), *aff'd. sub nom.* Benny v. Loew's, Inc., 239 F.2d 532 (9th Cir. 1956).

19. Columbia Pictures Corp. v. National Broadcasting Co., 137 F. Supp. 348, 350 (S.D. Cal. 1955).

20. *Ibid.*

21. Robert Stigwood Group, Ltd. v. O'Reilly, 346 F. Supp. 376 (D. Conn. 1972).

22. Time, Inc. v. Bernard Geis Associates, 293 F. Supp. 130 (S.D.N.Y. 1968).

23. Scherr v. Universal Match Corp. 297 F. Supp. 102 (S.D.N.Y. 1967)

24. Sony Corporation of America v. Universal City Studios, Inc., 27 P.T.C.J. 259, _____ U.S. _____, (1984).

25. H. Rep., p. 74.

26. *Ibid.*, p. 73.

27. Basic Books, Inc. v. Gnomon Corp., D. Conn. 1980, Civ. Action No. 80–36.

28. H. Rep., pp. 73–4.

29. *Ibid.*, pp. 68–70.

30. *Ibid.*, pp. 70–71.

31. H.R. Conf. Ref. No. 94–1733, 2nd Sess. 70, 1976 U.S. Code Cong. & Ad. News 5659, 5811.

32. 17 U.S.C. §108.

33. 17 U.S.C. §108(d).

34. Final Report of CONTU, pp. 54–55.

35. H. Rep., p. 77.

36. 17 U.S.C. §108(f)(1).

Chapter 9
1. Heim v. Universal Pictures Co., Inc., 154 F.2d 480 (2nd Cir. 1946).

2. Former Title 17 of the U.S. Code, §§19, 21.

3. L & L White Metal Casting Corp. v. Cornell Metal Specialties Corp., 353 F. Supp. 1170 (E.D.N.Y. 1972), *aff'd.* 177 U.S.P.Q. 673 (2nd Cir. 1973); First American Artificial Flowers, Inc. v. Joseph Markovits, Inc., 342 F. Supp. 178 (S.D.N.Y. 1972).

4. Copyrights Act of 1976, P. L. 94–553, §§103, 108.

5. Goodis v. United Artists Television, Inc., 425 F.2d 397 (2nd Cir. 1970).

6. Group Publishers v. Winchell, 86 F. Supp. 573, 576 (S.D.N.Y. 1952). However, this recordation requirement might well apply still to other types of works; see former Title 17 of the U.S. Code, §32.

7. Pushman v. New York Graphic Society, Inc., 287 N.Y. 302, 39 N.E.2d 249 (1942); Chamberlain v. Feldman, 300 N.Y. 135, 89 N.E.2d 863 (1949).

8. N.Y. Laws 1966, Ch. 688, §3; California Civ. Code, §982(e).

9. Picture Music, Inc. v. Bourse, Inc., 457 F.2d 1213 (2nd Cir. 1972). *Cf.*, Shapiro, Bernstein & Co. v. Jerry Vogel Music Co., 221 F.2d 569 (2nd Cir. 1955), *mod. on other grounds on rehearing* 223 F.2d 252 (2nd Cir. 1955).

10. Shapiro, Bernstein & Co., Inc. v. Jerry Vogel Music Co., Inc., *supra*; Donna v. Dodd, Mead & Co., Inc., 374 F. Supp. 429 (S.D.N.Y. 1974).

11. White-Smith Pub. Co. v. Apollo Co., *supra*.

12. *See, generally*, Nimmer, *op. cit.*, §2.10.

13. 17 U.S.C. §301(c).

14. Rosette v. Rainbo Record Mfg. Corp., 354 F. Supp. 1183 (S.D.N.Y. 1973), *aff'd* 546 F.2d 461 (2nd Cir. 1976). *See, generally*, Nimmer, *op. cit.*, §4.05.

15. Epoch Producing Corp. v. Killiam Shows, Inc., 522 F.2d 737 (2nd Cir. 1975).

16. Miller Music Company v. Chas. N. Daniels, Inc., 362 U.S. 373 (1960).

17. Fred Fisher Music Co. v. M. Witmark & Sons., 318 U.S. 643 (1943).

18. Marks Music Corp. v. Borst Music Pub. Co., 110 F. Supp. 923 (D.N.J. 1953).

19. De Sylva v. Ballentine, 351 U.S. 570 (1956); 17 U.S.C. §304(a), 101.

20. Rose v. Bourne, Inc., 279 F.2d 79 (2d Cir. 1960).

21. Edward B. Marks Music Corp. v. Jerry Vogel Music Company, 140 F.2d 266 (2nd Cir. 1944); *but see* Nimmer, *op. cit.*, §9.05[E].

22. Bartok v. Boosey & Hawkes, Inc., 523 F.2d 941 (2d Cir. 1975).

23. H.Rep., p. 139.

24. Former Title 17 of the U.S. Code, §24; *see* Shapiro, Bernstein & Co. v. Bryan, 123 F.2d 697 (2d Cir. 1941).

25. 17 U.S.C. §304(a).

26. 17 U.S.C. §408(c)(3).

27. 17 U.S.C. §304.

28. 17 U.S.C. §304(c).

29. *Ibid.*, 37 C.F.R. Ch.II, §201.10.

Chapter 10

1. Rev. Rul. 68–194, 1968–1 C.B. 87.

2. C. W. Churchman, 68 T.C. 696 (1977).

3. I.R.S. Pub. 334, Reg. §1.183–2.

4. Rev. Rul. 73–395, 1972–2 C.B. 87, as affected by P.L. 94–455, §2119. *See* Stern v. U.S.A., 1971–1 U.S.T.C. ¶86,491 (C.D. Cal. 1971).

5. Reg. §1.167(a)–1(b).

6. Rev. Rul. 60–358, 1960–2 C.B. 68.

7. *Ibid.*

8. Rev. Rul. 68–194, 1968–1 C.B. 87.

9. Reg. §1.167(a)–6(a); Rev. Rul. 73–395, 1973–2 C.B. 87, as affected by P.L. 94–455, §2119.

10. Heim v. Fitzpatrick, 262 F.2d 887 (2d Cir. 1959).

11. Rev. Rul. 55–706, 1955–2 C.B. 300.

12. This is by analogy to patents. See Reg. §1.1235–2(b)(2)(ii).

13. Cory v. Commissioner of Internal Revenue, 230 F.2d 941 (2d Cir. 1956), *cert. den.* 352 U.S. 828 (1956); for a patent analogy *see* Marco (1955), 25 T.C. 544.

14. Internal Revenue Code, §1014.

Chapter 11

1. For a detailed discussion of this, particularly as it affects works of the U.S. Government, *see* Ringer and Flacks, *op. cit.,* at pp. 157–204. The United States is excused from protecting French buildings to the extent that they are works of applied art.

2. Ringer and Flacks, *op. cit.,* at pp. 199–200.

3. U.C.C. Article III(1).

4. U.C.C. Article V(2).

5. U.C.C. Articles V(bis), V(ter), V(quater).

6. *See generally*, Nimmer, *op.cit.*, §17.04[D].

7. H. Rep., p. 168.

8. H. Rep., p. 169.

Index

Advertisements and labels
  deposit requirements for, 77, 81, 82
  as permissible display, 98
  as permissible performance, 97
  and separate notice, 61
Anonymous works, 39–40
Anthologies. *See* Compilations
Architectural works
  deposit requirements for, 77, 80
  and international protection of buildings, 175, 214
  scope of protection for, 15, 175, 214
  as works for hire, 29
Archives. *See* Library copying
Arrangements, as copyrightable works, 4, 116
Art works. *See* Pictorial works; Sculptural works
Attorney's fees. *See* Lawsuits
Audiovisual works
  deposit requirements for, 78, 79, 80, 81, 82, 83, 84–85
  as derivative works, 5
  and eligibility for copyright, 13
  and fixation at time of broadcast, 73, 84
  investment tax credit for, 169
  and "motion picture rights," 43
  and performance right, 93, 94–95, 135–136 (*see also* Videorecording; Educational use; Blind, deaf, and handicapped persons; Cable transmissions; Public broadcasting)
  and television programs, 78, 84–85, 139
Authorship. *See also* Joint authors; Works made for hire
  amateur vs. professional (*see* Taxation)
  definition of, 24
  and duration of copyright, 38–40
  and ownership, 24–38

Baker v. Selden, 11–12, 15
Berne Convention. *See* International copyright protection
Best edition, 78, 80
"Betamax" case. *See* Fair use
Blind, deaf, and handicapped persons
  copying for, 127
  exempt performances for, 94–95, 96–97
  Library of Congress license for, 87–88
  videotaping off-air for, 135–136
Broadcasting, 93. *See also* Audiovisual works; Cable transmissions; Public broadcasting; Videorecording
Buildings. *See* Architectural works
Burlesque. *See* Fair use

Cable transmissions, 108–111

Calligraphy, 14, 126–127
Characters. *See also* Dolls
  and eligibility for copyright, 16–18
  fair use of, 121–122
  ownership of, 16–18
Choreographic works, 2, 13, 59
Collages, 4, 34
Collective works. *See* Compilations
Commissioned works, 28–34
Common law copyright, 2–3, 57, 142
  suit regarding, 116
Community property, 37–38
Compilations. *See also* Educational
    use; Library copying
  anthologies as infringement, 127,
    130, 134–35
  authorship and ownership of, 34–35
  and contributions to collective works
    deposit requirements for, 77, 80
    licensing of, 43–44
    multiple registration for, 85–86
    multiple renewal of, 155
    notice requirements for, 61,
      144–145
  definition of, 32
  dictionaries and directories as, 32
  and eligibility for copyright, 8
  notice requirements for, 61, 144–145
Compulsory licenses. *See* Cable trans-
    missions; Jukeboxes; Phonore-
    cords; Public broadcasting
Computers, computer programs, com-
    puter music, and data bases
  computer music, 60–61
  deposit requirements for, 82,
    195–196
  and eligibility for copyright, 18–23
  and scope of protection, 18–23,
    90–92, 135
  and works created by computers
    authorship and ownership of, 23,
      35–36
Confidential materials, notice on,
    70–71
Contracts, suggested terms, 8, 17–18,
    40, 44–45, 48, 61, 63, 66, 88. *See
    also* Transfers of copyright

CONTU. *See* National Commission
Copyright
  as distinguished from patent, 1, 4,
    20
  as distinguished from trademark, 1
  requirements for, 1–2
  works eligible for, 12–16, 18–23
"Copyright owner," defined, 36, 62.
    See also Ownership; Transfers of
    copyright
Copyright Royalty Tribunal, 106, 110
Criminal infringement, 119

Dance. *See* Choreographic works
Data bases. *See* Computers
Deaf persons. *See* Blind, deaf, and
    handicapped persons
Deposit. *See* Library of Congress;
    Registration
Derivative works
  definition of, 4–5
  and eligibility for copyright, 4–10
  of public domain material, 5
  rights of author of, 5, 9–10, 92
  under old law, 145
  after statutory termination of grant,
    49, 162
Designs. *See also* Pictorial works
  deposit requirements for, 77, 82
  scope of protection for, 15–16
Dictionaries. *See* Compilations
Directories. *See* Compilations
Display. *See also* Educational use of
    'copyrighted works
  definition of, 58
  notice not required, 57
  public broadcasting compulsory
    license for, 111–112
  right of, 36–37, 97–98
Divisibility. *See* Ownership
Dolls and toys
  as derivative works, 4, 92
  deposit requirements for, 77, 82
Dramatic works. *See* Performance
Droit de suite, 99–100
Duration of copyright. *See* Term of
    copyright

Editors and editorial matter. *See*
   Revisions
Educational use of copyrighted works
   and display, 98, 121, 135
   and duplication of phonorecords,
      134
   and performance, 94, 135
   and photocopying
      of literary works, 128–133
      of musical works, 133–135
      of notice requirement, 132
      of pictorial works, 128–133
      of unpublished works, 132
   and videotaping off-air, 133, 135
Expression
   computer programs as, 21–23
   as distinguished from idea, 10–12
   plots, characters, and locale as,
      16–18
   and copyrightability, 2, 10

Facts, uncopyrightability of, 3
Fair use, 119–136. *See also* Educa-
      tional use; Infringement; Library
      copying
   and commercial copying, 127–128
   copying for blind person as, 127
   criticism and scholarly quotation as,
      120–121
   definition of, 120–121
   and freedom of speech, 122–124
   news reporting as, 120, 123–124
   parody as, 121–122
   personal use as, 124–127, 132
   photocopying as, 119–120
   videorecording as, 124–126, 135, 139
Fakes, 115
Families of authors
   ownership of copyright by, 53–56,
      158–160
   renewal rights of, 150–155
   termination by, 49–56, 157–161
First Amendment, 122–124
Fixation, 1–3, 57
Foreign publication. *See also* Manufac-
      turing clause

notice not required for, 142
registration and deposit of, 75, 81
Forms, 11–12
Freedom of speech and religion. *See*
   First Amendment

Games, 77, 82
Gifts. *See* Taxation; Transfers of
   copyright
Globes. *See* Maps and globes
Grants *See* Transfers of copyright
Graphics. *See* Pictorial works

Handicapped persons. *See* Blind, deaf,
   and handicapped persons
Hire, works made for. *See* Works
   made for hire
Holmes, Justice Oliver Wendell, 116
Holograms, 79, 83

Ideas, 3, 10–12. *See also* Expression
Infringement, 113–140. *See also* Fair
   use; Lawsuits; Photocopying
   and defective notice, 64–65, 69–70
Inheritance. *See* Taxation
Injunctions. *See* Lawsuits
International copyright protection,
   173–177

Jewelry, 77, 82
Joint authors
   definition of, 25–28
   and duration of copyright, 26, 39
   under pre-1978 law, 147–148
   renewal by, 153
   tax allocation among, 168
   termination of transfers by, 50–51,
      158
Jukeboxes, 105–108

Lawsuits. *See also* Infringement
   attorney's fees, 72, 118–119
   damages, 72, 117–119, 165
   entitlement to sue, 117–118
   for infringement by cable, 111
   injunctions, 119

Lawsuits (continued)
  and recordation, 48
  and registration, 72
  tax considerations, 165
  time requirements, 116–117
Letters, 59
Library of Congress
  deposit for, 76–80, 83
  and special nonexclusive license,
    87–88
Library copying, 136–140
  and off-air videotaping, 139
Licenses. See Compulsory licenses;
    Transfers of copyright
Limited publication. See Publication
Literary works, 13, 73, 75, 77, 78. See
    also Manufacturing clause

Magazines. See Compilations
"Maltese Falcon" case, 16–18
Manufacturing clause, 177–179
Maps and globes. See also Pictorial
    works
  deposit requirements for, 79, 80
  and eligibility for copyright, 13
Mathematical equations, 3
Misappropriation, 13–14
"Moral right," 99–100
Motion pictures. See Audiovisual
    works
Musical works. See also Educational
    use; Performance; Phonorecords
  and computer music, 60–61
  deposit requirements for, 77, 78, 79,
    81, 82, 83
  fixation of, 2
  as joint works, 24–27
  jukebox license for, 105–108
  notice on, 59–61, 62, 63
  orchestrations as derivative works of,
    4
  public broadcasting license for,
    111–112
  sound recordings as derivative works
    of, 4

National Commission on New Tech-
    nological Uses of Copyrighted
    Works (CONTU), 19–22, 138
News reporting. See Fair use; Library
    copying
Notice of copyright
  defects in, 63–66
  in deposit of identifying materials,
    84, 195–196
  elements of, 61–63
  for international protection, 61, 63,
    176
  need for, 57–61, 129, 132, 134
  on confidential materials, 70–71
  omission of, 66–70
  placement of, 62–63
  on pre-1978 works, 142–146, 148

Orchestrations. See Musical works
Originality, 1, 2, 3–10, 114
Ownership, 24–40. See also Author-
    ship; Joint authors; Transfers of
    copyright; Works made for hire
  and community property, 37–38
  of copy vs. of copyright, 37, 146
  divisibility of, 36–37
  indivisibility of, 144–146
  pre-1978 law, 144–148
  for registration purposes, 73

Paintings. See Pictorial works
Pantomimes, 2, 13. See also Dramatic
    works
Parody. See Fair use
Patent, 1, 4, 20
Performance
  definition of, 58, 93
  compared to publication, 58
  right of, 93
    exceptions to, 94–97, 121
    compulsory licenses of, 105–112
  subject to copyright, 2, 13
Periodicals. See Compilations
Personal use. See Fair use
Phonorecords. See also Sound
    recordings

compulsory license for, 73, 101–105
and computer music, 60–61
definition of, 59–60
"Harry Fox" license for, 105
notice on, 59–62
and pre-1978 law, 148–149
Photocopying. See Educational use of
      copyrighted works; Fair use; Li-
      brary copying
Photographs. See also Pictorial works
as fair use, 124
infringement of, 116
international protection of, 174–175
Pictorial works. See also Collages; De-
      signs; Display
composition of, 116
and eligibility for copyright, 13
as joint works, 27–28
and notice requirement, 58, 61, 67
registration and deposit of, 73, 77,
      79, 80, 81, 82, 83
sale of, as publication, 58
tax problems concerning, 167–168
Plots
as expression, 16
fair use of, 114, 121–122
Posthumous works. See Renewal
Preemption, 14n.21
Pre-1978 works, 141–162. See also
      particular topics
Pre-prints, 58
Processes, 1
Pseudonymous works, 39–40
Publication, 57–59, 61–62. See also
      Common law copyright; Foreign
      publication
Public broadcasting compulsory li-
      cense, 48, 111–112

Radio. See Broadcasting
Recordation. See Lawsuits; Tranfers of
      copyright
Registration, 72–89
certificate of, 88–89
corrections of, 86–87
as cure for inadequate notice, 64, 66,
      72

deposit for, 73, 76, 79–85
fee, 76
forms, 73–74
multiple, 85–86
as prerequisite to compulsory
      phonorecord license, 73
as prerequisite to suit, 72
Renewal, 149–162
application for, 149–155
of group of works, 155
of joint works, 153
and length of term, 149, 155–156
ownership after, 150–154
ownership of right to, 149–150
of posthumous works, 153–154
termination of grants concerning,
      156–162
of works made for hire, 154
Revisions, 6–8

Scientific discoveries, 3
Sculptural works
deposit requirements for, 77, 82
and eligibility for copyright, 13
notice on, 63, 67
sale of, as publication, 58
tax problems concerning, 167–168
Slogans, 1, 13
Songs. See Musical works
Sound Recordings. See also Educa-
      tional use
and deposit with Library of Con-
      gress, 75
as derivative works, 4
international protection of, 173
notice on publication of, 59–61
under pre-1978 law, 148–149
registration of, 73
scope of copyright in, 92, 93
Speeches, 58, 77, 80
State laws. See Common law copy-
      right; Preemption
Stationery, 77, 80
Style, imitation of, 115

Taxation, 163–172

Taxation (continued)
  and amateur vs. professional author,
    164
  basis for acquired copyright,
    169–170
  copyright as capital asset, 164–168,
    169–172
  of damages for infringement, 165
  deduction of expenses and losses,
    164–166, 167–168
  depreciation, 166–167, 171–172
  gift and estate taxes, 168–169, 170
  of joint authors, 168
  sale vs. license as affecting, 170–171
Television programs. See Audiovisual
    works; Fair use; Library copying
Termination of transfers. See Renewal;
    Transfers of copyright
Term of copyright, 38–40. See also
    Renewal
  for pre-1978 works, 141, 149–150,
    155–166
Tests
  deposit requirement for, 78, 81
  educational photocopying of, 130,
    134
Textiles, 77, 81
Theories, 3, 10
Titles, 1, 13
Toys. See Dolls and toys
Trademarks, 1, 13
  and use in copyright notice, 62, 142
Transfers of copyright, 41–56. See also
    Contracts.
  after termination, 53–56
  after termination of renewal (see
    Renewal)
  common law oral and implied, 30,
    42, 146
  conflicting, 46–48
  exclusive vs. nonexclusive, 42–44
  form of, 44–45
  involuntary, 41
  under pre-1978 law, 30, 42, 144–146
  recordation of, 45–48, 145
    as prerequisite to change in notice,
      145

  as prerequisite to suit, 48
  and renewal term (see Renewal)
  taxation of, 168–169, 170–171
  termination of, under statute, 49–53
Translations
  as derivative works, 4
  international protection of, 175–176
  scope of rights in, 9
Trivial works, 13
"12th Street Rag" doctrine, 147–148
Typefaces, 14

Unfair competition, 13–14. See also
    Preemption
United States Government, works of
  definition of, 30–31
  special notice requirement for use of,
    62, 66
  international protection of, 175n.1
Universal Copyright Convention. See
    International copyright protection
Unpublished works. See also Common
    law copyright; Educational use
  deposit requirements for, 81, 82,
    84–85
  international protection of, 174, 175
  protection of, 58–59
Utilitarian articles
  copyrighted works reproduced on
    deposit requirements for, 77, 81
  notice requirements for, 61
  definition of, 13–16, 77
  ineligibility for copyright, 13–16
  international protection of, 175n.1

Videorecording. See Educational use;
    Fair use
Visual works. See Pictorial works;
    Sculptural works

Works made for hire
  commissioned works as, 31–34
  definition of, 28–29
  duration of copyright in, 39
  employer-employee relationship in,
    29–31

ineligible for joint works, 39
ineligible for termination, 49, 157
and pre-1978 law, 146–147, 154
renewal of, 154
U.S. Government works as, 30–31